泾渭交汇

汉阳陵考古陈列馆

汉阳陵帝陵外藏坑保护展示厅基本陈列
荣获第七届（2005-2006年度）
全国博物馆十大陈列展览精品评选

精品奖

国家文物局

中国文物报社　中国博物馆学会

2007年5月

1999 年 6 月 16 日江泽民主席在汉阳陵考古发掘工地视察工作
Chairman Jiang Zemin inspecting the exavation work of Han Yangling on June 16,1999
1999 年 6 月 16 日江沢民主席が漢陽陵考古発掘現場を視察していた

En Témoignage d'estime et d'admiration
pour l'exceptionnel et remarquable Travail
des archéologues chinois au service de
l'histoire et de la culture du monde.

J. CHIRAC
28 octobre 2006

对为世界文明和历史作出杰出贡献的中国考古工作者由衷地表示敬佩和敬意

法国总统希拉克在参观汉阳陵地下博物馆后题词
French President Jacques Chirac giving inscription after visiting
the Han Yangling Underground Museum.
フランス共和国シラク大統領は漢陽陵地下博物館を見学
した後、考古学者に題詞した

汉 阳 陵 博 物 馆

Han Yangling Museum

汉阳陵博物馆　编

文物出版社

Cultural Relics Press

策　　划：焦南峰　　孙振江　　晏新志
　　　　　　吴晓丛　　李居西　　斐珺旻
　　　　　　曹发展　　颜宗岳
主　　编：王保平
副 主 编：马永赢　　李　岗　　李　库
撰　　文：吴晓丛　　王保平　　李　库
　　　　　　李曼丽　　石　宁　　白冬梅
　　　　　　何　倩　　程艳妮　　陈　波
摄　　影：王保平
英文翻译：赵利成　　余大虎　　何宇鹏
　　　　　　刘　军　　程艳妮
日文翻译：韩　钊　　周　瑞
法文翻译：黄传根　　Marie Denise Dal
装帧设计：张希广
责任印制：张道奇
责任编辑：郭维富

图书在版编目（ＣＩＰ）数据

汉阳陵博物馆／王保平主编. －北京：文物出版
社，2007.10（2009 重印）
ISBN 978-7-5010-2332-5

Ⅰ.汉…　Ⅱ.王…　Ⅲ.汉墓－考古发掘－咸阳市－西汉时代
Ⅳ.K878.84

中国版本图书馆 CIP 数据核字（2007）第 156365 号

汉阳陵博物馆

汉阳陵博物馆 编

文物出版社出版发行
(北京东直门内北小街 2 号　邮政编码 100007)
http://www.wenwu.com
E-mail:WEB@wenwu.com
北京画中画印刷有限公司制版印刷
新华书店经销
开本：889×1194　1/16　印张：8.75
2007 年 10 月第 1 版　2009 年 7 月第 2 次印刷
ISBN 978－7－5010－2332－5

目 录

序言

汉景帝刘启（公元前188年～前141年）是西汉王朝第四位皇帝。虽说较其祖父高祖刘邦及其子武帝刘彻，既缺乏大风一曲、慷慨卓绝的气概，也没有开边拓土、勒石燕然的雄健。然而，史家笔下以及后人心目中的刘启，应该算是一个圣明君主。他登基之后，承"黄老之术"，顺天应命，抚驭万民，和亲匈奴，轻徭薄赋，减笞去刑，与民生息，无为而治，的确颇有一番可嘉的实绩。质诸当时社会经济发展的有关史实来看，所谓"周云成康，汉言文景"的赞誉，也并非史家曲笔谀世之词，而"文景之治"也就成为后人心目中封建社会早期治国安邦的黄金时代。

阳陵是景帝刘启与其皇后王氏同茔异穴的合葬陵园，始建于公元前153年，至公元前126年基本告竣，历时约28年，在咸阳原上的西汉帝陵群中位居最东。这里地势高亢平坦，风水极佳，泾河蜿蜒于北，渭水奔腾于南，两河在陵东不远处交汇，形成挟双龙而东向的气势和"泾渭分明"的独特景观。在苍凉厚重的黄土台地的衬托下，显得格外突兀雄浑。虽说经过2150多年来兵燹战乱和风雨雷电的破坏，阳陵陵园原有的殿宇建筑基本荡然无存，但是，历史的积淀和岁月的洗礼，更造就出了汉阳陵"西风残照，汉家陵阙"的壮阔。

对于汉阳陵的考古调查始于20世纪70年代，1990年以后，伴随着咸阳国际机场专用公路的修建，考古工作者开始对这里进行大规模的清理和考古勘探。此后，在大约20平方公里的陵园范围内，便不断有一些世所瞩目的考古发现。现已初步探明，汉阳陵主要由帝陵陵园、后陵陵园、南北区从葬坑、礼制建筑、陪葬墓园、刑徒墓地以及阳陵邑等几部分组成。帝陵坐西朝东，被80余条呈放射状的陪葬坑簇拥着。其四周则等距离分布着后陵、南北区从葬坑以及建筑基址。宽约110米的司马道平坦如砥，向东延伸7华里直达陵邑——那里曾是富豪云集、商贾出没的繁华所在。而司马道两侧又密密匝匝排列着王侯将相和文武百官的陪葬墓园，一如当年天子临朝时大臣位列两班的威仪。众多陪葬坑内，一列列武士俑披坚执锐，征尘未洗，如临大敌；一排排仕女俑宽衣博带，美目流盼，舞姿翩翩；成群成组的猪、马、牛、羊、狗、鸡等动物陶塑密密匝匝，累千上万，排列有序。于是，徜徉其间，我们能真切地感受到，那些风干的历史一下子变得鲜活了，千年尘封的人事仿佛又从泛黄的线装书中摇摇曳曳走了出来。

中国历代帝王多信奉"事死如生"的礼制，秦汉之际，帝王为自己建造陵墓的热情更是达到空前的程度。所谓宫室之量、器皿之度、棺椁之厚、丘封之大，常令后世咋舌。从已经公布的考古资料看，应该说，在西汉帝王陵园的考古发掘、勘探调查和研究工作中，汉阳陵是目前工作最为深入周详，成果最为显著的一个。这些考古研究成果，正在为学术界所广泛关注和引用，成为科学工作者破解西汉帝王陵寝制度和丧葬文化的重要资料。

1999年，在考古发掘、勘探与研究的基础上，汉阳陵考古陈列馆落成。也许，仅就目前的建筑规模而言，它还不能和一些大型综合类历史博物馆相比，但是，由于紧密依托于帝王陵园和考古发掘现场之上，加之与历史生态环境的和谐统一，汉阳陵考古陈列馆已经或正在日益凸显出自己与众不同的特色和魅力。最新建成的帝陵外藏坑遗址保护展示厅，建筑面积7856多平方米，是我国第一座全地下的遗址博物馆。按照汉阳陵文物保护和利用的总体规划，通过对汉代文物资源的重新整合，一个更大规模的汉文化综合展览大厅也将于近年内在这里建成，从而构成汉阳陵博物馆的基本规模和框架。所有这些，使我们有充分的理由相信，在不久的将来，汉阳陵将不仅成为文物考古工作者的"天堂"，而且，在观赏领略大量出土文物精品的同时，身临其境地感受考古发掘和文物修复的真实场景，必定有助于激发起普通参观者寻幽探胜的极大热情，使汉阳陵成为国内外著名的观光胜地。

吴晓丛

2004年8月3日

PREFACE

Jing Di Emperor named Liu Qi (188 BCE ~ 141 BCE), was the fourth emperor in the Western Han Dynasty. Compared with his grand father Gao Zu (Liu Bang) and his son Wu Di (Liu Che), he was neither a man who founded a new empire nor someone who extended the territory of the nation. But he has been described by the historians as a beneficent ruler who believed the "Taoism" and ruled people by "doing nothing against the nature". After he ascended the throne, Jing Di made peace with Xiongnu (nomads to the north also known as the Huns), and reduced the people's tax and labor duties to the government, and lessened the cruel punishments of the law. In the Chinese history, the period during the rule of Wen Di (Jing Di's father) and Jing Di of the Han Dynasty has been regarded as the golden age in the imperial China.

Yangling is the tomb area shared by Jing Di and his Empress Wang. The project started in 153 BC and was completed in 126 BC lasting 28 years. Among all the Han imperial mausoleums on the Xianyang Highland, Yangling is the easternmost one. With Jing River running to the north and Wei River to the south, an aerial view of the Yangling looks as if two powerful dragons are protecting the imperial mausoleum on the two sides. After 2150 years of wartime destruction and weathering, the buildings above ground around the mausoleum have mostly disappeared and only the massive tomb mounds and the remnants in the field at the sunset can remind people of the prosperity of this area in the old days.

The archaeological investigation on Yangling started in the 1970s. Since 1990, when the highway to the airport was built passing by Yangling, the archaeologists have been clearing up the construction sites and digging around the tomb area of 20 square kilometers. Constant archaeological discoveries have brought the attention of the world to Yangling. The initial explorations have found Yangling to be composed of the Emperor's tomb area, the Empress' tomb area, the southern section of burial pits containing clay figures, the northern section of pits with clay figures, ritual and ceremonial buildings, satellite tombs, prisoners' graveyard, and the Yangling county, etc. The emperor's tomb, facing the east, is surrounded by 80 plus underground pits radiating from the center of the tomb mound. Around the Emperor's tomb, in equal distance, there are the Empress' tomb, the southern and northern sections of burial pits with clay figures, and the remains of the buildings. A 110 meter wide sacred path about 3.5 km long leads to the Yangling county, a small town that used to be very prosperous with rich merchants and nobles living there to keep company of the emperor's spirit. On two sides of the sacred path there are a great number of satellite tombs of the nobles and high officials representing the court audience of the subjects with the Emperor. Buried in the underground pits, rows of warriors holding weapons in their hands and clad in heavy armor are ready to sacrifice their own lives at any time for the safety of the emperor; thousands of young ladies in their beautiful silk dress are dancing elegantly; hordes of pigs, horses, cattle, sheep, goats, dogs, and chickens are packed together for the use of the emperor feasting. Suddenly, those petrified fragments of history have come to life, and the men and women thousands of years ago seem to have risen from the dusty and worn pages of the history books trying to tell us their stories.

All the Chinese emperors had the belief that people would go to live in an afterlife world when they died so that they wanted to bring everything in their life time to the after life. During the time of Qin and Han Dynasties, the enthusiasm of the emperors for building their tombs had reached its highest point. People are usually shocked by the size of the underground palace, the quantity of the funeral objects, the quality of the casket, and the massiveness of the tomb mound of the emperors' mausoleums from this period of time. Based on the archaeological materials that have been released to the public, among all the Han imperial mausoleums, the excavation, research and survey work at Yangling is the most complete and outstanding one. These achievements have been widely recognized and quoted by the archaeologists for better and further understanding of the ritual protocols of the imperial funeral and the burial culture in the Western Han Dynasty.

In 1999, based on the excavation and research work at the Yangling Mausoleum, the Han Yangling Archaeological Museum was established. Though in size it still cannot be compared with other large museums, the uniqueness of the Yangling Museum is that it is still growing. The Exhibition Hall of Burial Pits is a 7856-square-meter underground museum based on the pits around the tomb of the emperor. It is the first underground, on-the-site museum in China. According to the general plan of the protection and application of the historical remains at Yangling, a larger exhibition space of the Han culture will be built in a few years as part of the Han Yangling Museum. All of these have made us believe that in the near future the Han Yangling will not only be the paradise for the archaeologists but also the place for the visitors to experience the excavation and repairing work of the archaeologists. We are confident that Han Yangling will be one of the best tourist attractions both in China and in the world.

Wu Xiaocong
2004.8.3

はじめに

漢 の景帝劉啓（紀元前188年～紀元前141年）は前漢王朝第四代の皇帝である。彼の祖父劉邦に比べると、彼は大風一曲、慷慨卓絶（荒波のようであり、慷慨的である）といった英雄的気概を持っておらず、また、息子武帝劉徹のようにパイオニア精神と雄大さを兼ね備えた逞しさもなかった。しかし、歴史家が書き記し後世の人々に伝わる劉啓は、歴然たる君主であると言って間違いない。彼は即位した後、歴史の潮流に乗り「黄老之術」を継承し、民をやさしく保護し、匈奴との縁組、税の軽減、法の緩和、民への負担の軽減、無為而治（不干渉による支配）を実行することにより、確実にすばらしい実績を残したのである。当時の社会経済の発展に関する史実によると、「周云成康、漢言文景」と称えられており、歴史家がこびへつらって書いたのではなく、「文景之治」を行うことにより、後世の人々の心に残る封建社会早期に穏やかに国を治め、黄金時代を築いたのである。

陽陵は、漢の景帝と王皇后が合葬された陵園である。紀元前153年に建設が始められ、28年の歳月を要して紀元前126年に竣工した。ただし両者の墓室は別になっている。陽陵は咸陽台地にある前漢皇帝陵の中でもっとも東に位置する。この土地は高くなだらかな地形であり、風水もよく、泾河が北に位置し延々と続き、渭水が南に位置し勢いよく流れている。泾河と渭水は陵園の東のほど近い場所で交わり、陽陵は二本の川の間にあり、二匹の龍を携え東へと向かう勢いある情景と「泾渭分明」と呼ばれる独特の景観を形成している。見渡す限り荒涼としている黄土台地に際立ち、とりわけ雄渾な形で聳え立っているのである。建設から2150年以上の時間が経過し、人による戦乱戦火や自然界の雨風により破壊されて、陽陵陵園の廟などの建物、建築物は跡形もなく消え去ってしまったが、歴史の積み重ねと歳

月を経ることにより、漢陽陵の「西風残照、漢家陵闕（漢の陵墓が西からの風が吹かれ、夕日に照らされている美しい情景）」といった雄大でありながら時代の移り変わりをあらわした様子を作り出している。

漢の陽陵の考古調査は20世紀の70年代に始められた。1990年以降、咸陽国際空港専用道路の建設と同時に、考古学者はここの大規模な整備を行うとともに発掘研究を進めた。その後、約20平方キロメートルの陵園の範囲にわたり、世の注目を集める考古学上の発見が、相次いでいる。現在まで既に、漢陽陵の主要部分は、帝陵陵園、后陵陵園、南北区の従葬坑、礼制建築、陪葬墓園、罪人の墓地や陽陵邑などのいくつかの部分から成り立っていることが解明されている。帝陵は東向きで陵園の西に位置しており、放射状に八十本あまりの副葬坑（副葬品を埋納した溝）に囲まれている。帝陵の周囲四方には等間隔で后陵、南北の副葬坑と建築遺跡が分布している。幅約110メートルの司馬道は平坦で東に向かって伸び3.5キロメートルあり、陵邑へと直接つながっている。そこは富豪が集まっていた地区で、商売なども行われていた繁華街である。また、司馬道の両側は王公貴族や文武官の陪葬陵園がぎっしりと並び、当時のように皇帝が執政する時の大臣が両側に並び執政する威厳ある等級概念を明確にしている。多くの陪葬坑の中には、武士俑が武装し遠征から戻った汚れもまだ落としておらず、大敵に臨む姿で並べられている。仕女俑は、ゆったりとした衣服をまとい幅の広い帯をつけ、美しい流し目をしており、軽やかに舞っている。また、豚、馬、牛、羊、犬、鶏などの動物俑が、ぎっしりと配列され風も通さないほどに密集している。実際にそこを歩いてみると、遠い昔の歴史が鮮やかに甦ってくるのが実感でき、千年の埃に埋もれた人々、事柄が彷彿と甦ってくるとともにほころびた古籍の中の世界をさまよっているようである。

中国歴代帝王の多くは「事死如生（死後も生存中の世界と同じように）」の礼儀、制度を信じ、特に秦漢の時には、帝王は自らの陵墓の建設に力を注ぎ空前の規模の陵墓を生み出した。墓室の数が多く、器の品質もすばらしい。内棺、外棺ともに厚く作られており、古墳の土盛は部分大きく後世の人々は舌を巻いた。すでに発表されている考古資料からもわかるように、前漢帝王の陵園考古発掘、調査研究は、漢の陽陵は今日まで念入りに進められ、発掘、研究の成果が最も顕著である陵墓のひとつである。これらの考古研究の成果は、学界において広範な注目を浴び、科学者により前漢の帝王陵の陵園制度と墓葬文化が明らかにされ、重要な資料となっている。

考古の発掘、研究に基づき、1999年漢陽陵考古陳列館は、正式に落成した。現時点の建築規模は、大型の総合歴史博物館とは比べ物にはならないが、帝王の陵園、考古発掘現場と一体となっているのに加え、歴史的環境が調和されたことにより、漢陽陵考古陳列館はすばらしい博物館となり、多くの他の博物館にはない特色と魅力を兼ね備えています。最新にじまた帝陵外藏坑遺跡保護展示棟は建築面積約7856平方メートルあり、わが国で初の地下遺跡博物館である。また、漢陽陵博物館の総合計画に基づき、漢代文物を整理し、さらに規模の大きな漢文化総合展覧大展示棟も近年中に建設することになっている。これらすべては来館者を納得させるものであり、近い将来漢陽陵は文物、考古の専門家の「天国」になることだろう。また大量の出土遺物を見学できる以外にも考古発掘と文物修復の実際の現場を体感できる。一般参観者を魅了することは間違いなく、漢陽陵は国内外の著名な観光地になることが期待される。

吳曉叢
2004年8月3日

INTRODUCTION

L'Empereur Liu Qi, portant le titre de Jing Di (188-141BC) était le 4ème empereur de la Dynasty Han de l'Ouest. Si on le compare à son grand-père Gao Zu (Liu Bang) où à son fils Wu Di (Liu Che), il n'était ni un homme capable de fonder un nouvel empire, ni un homme capable d'étendre son térritoire. Cependant il a été descrit par les historiens comme un souverain plein de sagesse appliquant les règles Taoistes, qui consistaient à « ne rien faire contre la nature ». Il était considéré comme un empereur plein d'èsprit et de sagesse.

Apres son ascenssion au trône, Jing Di fit de son mieux pour améliorer les relations avec les Xiongnu (nomades du nord connus également sous le nom de Huns), en arrangeant des marriages avec les princesses de la noblesse de son royaume. Il réduisit les taxes et les obligations due par le peuple au gouvernement, ainsi que les pénalités imposées aux condamnés par la loi. Dans l'histoire chinoise, la période de la Dynasty Han comprenant le règne de Wen Di (le père de Jing Di) et celui de Jing Di lui-meme, a été regardée comme l'age d'or de l'impérialisme chinois.

Yangling est le lieu d'enterrement de l'Empereur LIU QI et de sa femme l'imperatrice WANG, bien que les deux tombes soient séparés.

Le Mausolée a été construit en 28 ans, entre 153 et 126BC. De tous les Mausolées de la dynasty Han de l 'Ouest construits sur la colline de Xianyang, Yangling est le plus à l'Est. Xianyang est un plateau baigné par les rivières Jing au nord et Wei au sud. Ces rivières se rencontrent à l'est du Mausolée de Yangling. Une vue aériènne de Yangling les font apparaitre comme deux dragons protègeant les tombes impériales.

Après 2150 ans de guerre et de destructions par les

intempéries, les bâtiments sur le terrains ont pratiquement disparus. Seuls restent des monticules qui rappellent cependant la prospèrite de cette région et son prestigieux passé.

Les travaux archéologiques de Yangling ont démarrés au début des années 70 (au 20ème siècle). Après la construction de l'autoroute conduisant à l'aéroport en 1990 et la découverte d'objects anciens dans les environs de Yangling, les archéologistes ont commencé une fouille sur une surface de 20km2, qui a mis à jour des découvertes importantes. Le cimetière de Yangling est composé de la tombe de l'Empereur et de celle de l'Impératrice ainsi que de plusieurs autres tombes pour mandarins. Le mausolée de l'Empereur est tournée vers l'Est et est entourée de 80 tombes situees en rayon autour de sa tombe. D'autres batiments sont alignés à distance régulière tout autour. La voie sacrée de 3.5km de long et d'une largeur de 110m, s'étend vers l'Est en direction de l'ancien centre de commerce de l'époque des Hans de l'Ouest.

Le long de cette voie sont alignés les tombes de princes et princesses, mandarins et généraux ainsi que de guerriers avec leur arme à la main et de jeunes femmes au maquillage soigné et au geste élégant ainsi que d'un nombre important d'animaux domestiques divers, en terre cuite tels que des chevaux, des moutons, des porcs, des chiens, des coqs etc, tous entassés là pour servir de nourriture à l'Empereur. Il semble que tous ces objects pétrifiés par le temps veuillent sortir de leur long sommeil pour nous raconter leur histoire.

Tous les Empereurs chinois voyaient la mort comme une renaissance. C'est pour cette raison qu'ils voulaient emporter avec eux tous les object de leur vie terrestre. Durant le règne des Qui et des Han la construction de

tombes grandioses par les Empereurs, a atteint une grandeur jamais vue avant cette époque. L'envergure du cimetière, la taille importante des tombes et l'épaisseur des sarcophages ainsi que la diversité des objects trouvés, tout à causé une surprise énorme. Parmi tous les documents archéologiques publiés sur toutes les tombes impériales, les fouilles de Yangling sont les plus complètes et les plus importantes. Ces recherches sont vraiment une « première » et trés importantes pour la connaissance des rituels funéraires de la dynastie des Hans occidentaux.

En 1999, sur la base des recherches et découvertes faites au cimetière de Yangling, le musée archéologique de Han Yangling a été fondé. Bien que sa petite taille ne puisse permettre de le comparer à d'autres musées plus larges, sa situation unique – sur le site même des tombes – est en harmonie parfaite avec son environnement. Le Musée des Tombes de Yangling est le premier musée souterrain de la Chine. Construit directement sur les fausses, ce musée couvre une surface de 7856m2 et est situé à coté de la tombe de l'Empereur. C'est le premier musée chinois souterrain. Suivant le future plan d'extension, le musée sera developpé pour abriter une exposition des objects de tous genres découverts, au fur et à mesure des fouilles

On a toutes raisons de croire que dans le proche future, le musée archéologique de Yangling sera, non seulement le « paradis » des archéologistes chinois et étrangers, mais aussi un lieu de grand intérêt pour les visiteurs qui pourront,de leur propres yeux, decouvrir l'intérêt de ces excavations et le mystère du tumulus de Yangling. Il ne fait aucun doute que ce lieu est destiné a devenir célèbre dans le monde entier

Wu Xiaocong
2004.8.3

一、气势雄浑壮阔的汉阳陵

汉阳陵位于古城西安以北咸阳渭城区张家湾村北原上，雄居五陵原东端。东眺泾渭交汇之地，西与汉高祖的长陵遥遥相望。陵园内，帝陵与后陵两座巨大的覆斗形陵冢比肩而立。帝陵在西，高约31米，后陵在东，高约25.5米。两者间距450米。封土下是皇帝和皇后的陵寝，形制为四条墓道的亚字形大墓。封土外围放射状分布着从葬坑，帝陵81条，后陵28条。考古资料表明，汉阳陵是迄今发现的最为完整的西汉帝王陵园。其整齐规矩的陵邑、排列有序的从葬坑和陪葬墓园以及规模宏大的礼制性建筑，在中国古代陵墓建造的历史上极具典型性。通过对帝陵东侧北部11座从葬坑的发掘，出土了大量的动物陶塑、生活用具、粮仓、兵器、车马器、著衣式陶俑、粉彩仕女俑、宦官俑、玺印封泥等珍贵文物，形象地再现了西汉时期的宫廷文化。

1. 咸阳原上的汉阳陵
Han Yangling on the Xianyang Highland
咸陽原上漢陽陵

A. Grand Han Yangling

Han Yangling, built right on the eastern end of the Five Tomb Highland, is located on the Xianyang Highland in the northwest of Xi'an. To its east is the confluence of Jing and Wei Rivers and to its west in the distance is Changling mausoleum of Han Emperor Gao Zu. Two huge burial mounds of the Emperor and Empress stand close to each other in the tomb area. The Emperor's tomb is in the west with a 31m high burial mound while the Empress' tomb is in the east with a burial mound of 25.5m high. The tombs of the Emperor and Empress were all built with four ramps under the burial mounds. There are 81 burial pits radiating from the mound of the Emperor's tomb and 28 near the Empress' tomb. The archaeological data have proven that Han Yangling is the most intact imperial mausoleum of Western Han Dynasty ever found. Therefore, its well layout, regularly-built burial pits and satellite tombs as well as large-scale ritual buildings are quite typical in the construction of the royal tombs of ancient China. The excavation of 11 burial pits to the northeast of the Emperor's tomb has yielded a large number of relics such as pottery animals, daily necessities, miniature granaries, weapons, chariots and horses, clothed pottery figures, painted pottery girls, pottery eunuchs, chops, lute and many other valuable relics, vividly reproducing the imperial court culture of the Western Han Dynasty.

1. 雄大な気魂に迫る漢陽陵

漢陽陵は西安市の北方向咸陽渭城区張家湾村北の高い場所に位置し、五陵原の中でもっとも東に位置する。東は"泾渭の会"を臨み、西は漢高宗長陵と境を接する。陵園の皇帝陵と皇后陵は覆斗形を呈し対峙して並んでいる。皇帝陵は西にあり、高さ31メートル、皇后陵は東にあり、高さ25.2メートル、皇帝陵と皇后陵は450メートル離れている。封土の下には皇帝と皇后の寝室があり、4条の墓道が"亜"字型になっている。封土の外側に、放射状に分布している従葬坑が発見されており、中には帝陵が81個、皇后陵が28個ある。考古学発掘調査によると、漢陽陵は今まで発掘された中で最も完全にそろっている前漢の皇帝陵園である。陵園には陵邑が整い、従葬坑の配列も順序よく並び、従葬墓園及び陵廟など礼制建築は、中国古代陵園建築の中でもっとも代表的な陵園である。帝陵東側北部11個の従葬坑の発掘によって、人量の動物陶俑、生活用具、食糧、兵器、車馬具、着衣式陶俑、粉彩仕女俑、宦者俑、璽印封泥などの珍しい文物が出土され、前漢時期の宮廷文化が生き生きと再現されている。

2. 汉景帝阳陵陵园
A general view of Yangling Mausoleum
漢陽陵の陵園

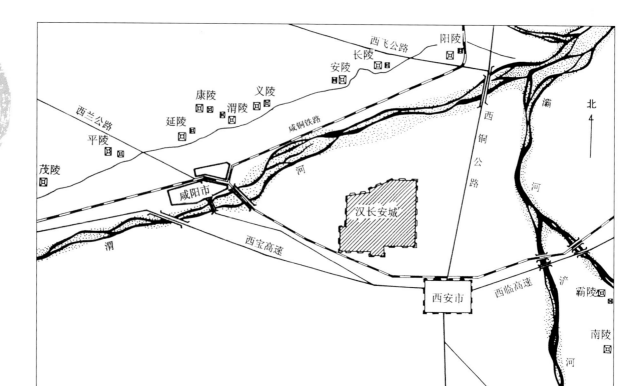

3. 汉阳陵地理位置图
The geographic location of
Han Yangling
漢陽陵位置図

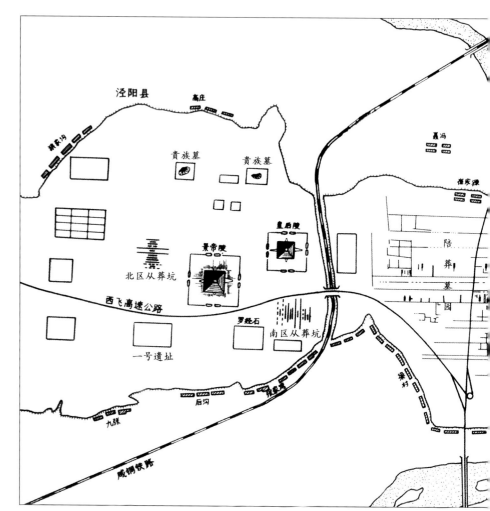

4. 汉阳陵陵区遗迹平面图
Plan map showing the distribution
of relics in Han Yangling
漢陽陵陵園遺跡の平面図

5．覆斗形的帝陵封土
Panorama of the Emperor's tomb
覆斗形を呈する帝陵封土

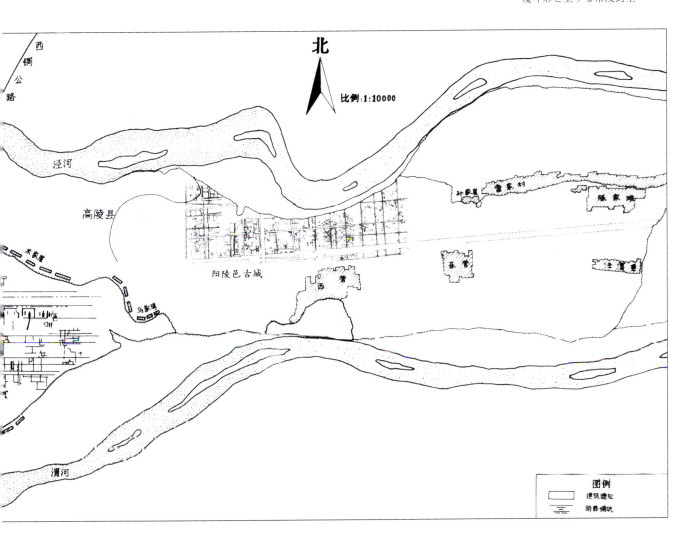

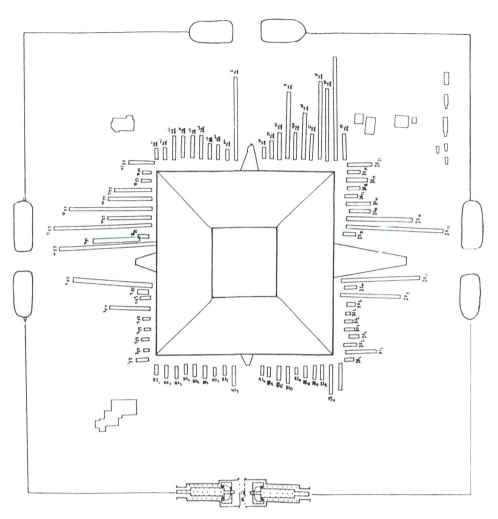

6. 帝陵陵园钻探平面图
Excavation map of the Emperor's tomb
帝陵陵園試掘平面図

7. 帝陵东侧12—21号坑发掘现场
Excavation sites of burial pit(pit12—21) to the east of the Emperor's tomb
帝陵東側従葬坑（12-21）

8. 帝陵东侧13号坑西区
   彩绘陶仓发掘现场
   Excavation site of the pottery
   granary in Pit 13 to the east of
   the Emperor's tomb
   色彩陶倉の発掘現場
   帝陵東側13号従葬坑

9. 帝陵东侧13号坑出土的彩绘陶乳猪
   Painted pottery piglets unearthed from Pit 13 to the east of the Emperor's tomb
   色彩陶子豚　帝陵東側13号従葬坑から出土

10. 帝陵东侧13号坑出土的彩绘陶狗
    Painted pottery dogs unearthed from Pit 13 to the east of the Emperor's tomb
    色彩陶犬　帝陵東側13号従葬坑から出土

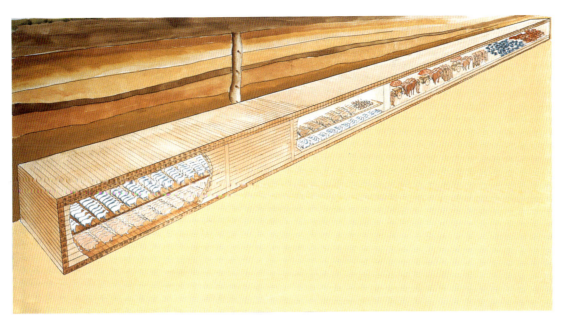

11. 帝陵东侧 13 号坑复原示意图
Sketch map of the restored Pit 13
to the east of the Emperor's tomb
帝陵の東側 13 号従葬坑復元図

12. 帝陵东侧 13 号坑出土的彩绘陶绵羊
Excavation site of the painted pottery sheep in Pit 13 to the east of Emperor's tomb
色彩陶绵羊　帝陵東側 13 号従葬坑から出土

13. 帝陵东侧 13 号坑出土的彩绘动物俑群全景
Panorama of the painted animals in Pit 13 to the east of
the Emperor's tomb
色彩陶の動物俑群　帝陵東側 13 号従葬坑から出土

14. 铜质"太官之印"印章
帝陵东侧 16 号坑出土　高 1.2、边长 0.9 厘米
Bronze seal of "Tai Guan"(an official title of the
Han) unearthed from Pit 16 to the east of the
Emperor's tomb
Height: 1.2cm　Length: 0.9cm
"太官之印"銅製印章
帝陵東側 16 号従葬坑から出土
高 1.2、边長 0.9cm

15. 帝陵东侧 13 号坑彩绘木车遗迹
Remains of the wooden chariot in Pit 13 to the east of the
Emperor's tomb
色彩木馬車遺跡　帝陵東側 13 号従葬坑発見

16. 帝陵东侧 11 号坑彩绘男骑兵出土现场
Site of the cavalrymen in Pit 11 to the east of the Emperor's tomb
色彩男騎兵の出土現場　帝陵東側 11 号従葬坑

17. 帝陵东侧 11 号坑朱红色木质车轮遗迹
Remains of the red wooden wheel in Pit 11 to the east of the Emperor's tomb
朱色木車輪遺跡　帝陵東側 11 号従葬坑発見

汉阳陵博物馆

18. 男骑兵俑头　帝陵东侧 11 号坑出土
Head of a cavalryman unearthed from Pit
11 to the east of the Emperor`s tomb
男騎兵俑の頭部
帝陵東側 11 号従葬坑から出土

19. 粉彩仕女陶俑　帝陵从葬坑出土
Painted female figures unearthed from the
burial pits of the Emperor`s tomb
粉彩女俑　帝陵従葬坑から出土

20. 宦官俑　帝陵东侧 18 号坑出土
高 57.5 厘米
Pottery eunuchs unearthed from Pit 18 to the
east of the Emperor`s tomb
Height: 57.5cm
宦者俑　帝陵東側 18 号従葬坑から出土
高 57.5cm

21. 鎏金虎头铜饰
　　帝陵东侧16号坑出土
　　长1.3、宽1.8、高1.5厘米
　　Gold-plated tiger head ornaments unearthed from Pit 16 to the east of the Emperor's tomb
　　Height: 1.5cm　Width: 1.8cm　Length: 1.3cm
　　鎏金虎頭銅飾
　　帝陵東側16号従葬坑から出土
　　高1.5、長1.3、幅1.8cm

22. 帝陵东侧21号从葬坑发掘现场
Excavation site of No. 21 burial pit
in the southern area of the Mausoleum
帝陵東側21号従葬坑の発掘現場

23. 彩绘陶绵羊　帝陵东侧13号坑出土、高37、长43厘米
Painted pottery sheep unearthed from Pit 13 to the east of the Emperor's tomb
Height: 37cm　Length: 43cm
色彩陶綿羊　帝陵東側13号従葬坑から出土
高37、長43cm

24. 彩绘陶山羊
帝陵东侧13号坑出土　高32、长40厘米
Painted pottery goats unearthed from Pit 13 to
the east of the Emperor's tomb
Height: 32cm　Length: 40cm
色彩陶羊　帝陵東側13号従葬坑から出土
高32、長40cm

汉阳陵博物馆

25. 彩绘陶乳猪　帝陵东侧13号坑出土　高5.6、长16厘米
Painted pottery piglet unearthed from Pit 13 to the east of the Emperor's tomb
Height: 5.6cm　Length: 16cm
色彩陶子豚　帝陵東側13号従葬坑から出土　高5.6、長16cm

26. 彩绘陶猪　帝陵东侧13号坑出土　高22.5、长44厘米
Painted pottery pig unearthed from Pit 13 to the east of the Emperor's tomb
Height: 22.5cm　Length: 44cm
色彩陶豚　帝陵東側13号従葬坑から出土　高22.5、長44cm

27. 彩绘陶母猪　帝陵东侧13号坑出土　高22.5、长41厘米
Painted pottery sow unearthed from Pit 13 to the east of the Emperor's tomb
Height: 22.5cm　Length: 41cm
色彩陶母豚　帝陵東側13号従葬坑から出土　高22.5、長41cm

汉阳陵博物馆

28. 彩绘陶狼犬　帝陵东侧 13 号坑出土　高 31、长 20.5 厘米
　　Painted pottery hound unearthed from Pit 13 to the east of the Emperor's tomb　Height: 31cm　Length: 20.5cm
　　色彩陶狼犬　帝陵東側 13 号従葬坑から出土　高 31、長 20.5cm

29. 彩绘陶家犬　帝陵东侧 13 号坑出土　高 30、长 21 厘米
　　Painted pottery dog unearthed from Pit 13 to the east of the Emperor's tomb　Height: 30cm　Length: 21cm
　　色彩陶犬　帝陵東側 13 号従葬坑から出土　高 30、長 21cm

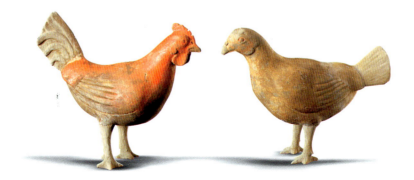

30. 彩绘陶鸡　帝陵东侧 15 号坑出土
　　Painted pottery chicken unearthed from Pit 15 to the east of the Emperor's tomb
　　色彩陶鶏　帝陵東側 15 号従葬坑から出土

32. **铜钵** 帝陵东侧21号坑出土
口径25、高10.2、沿宽0.6厘米
Bronze bowl unearthed from Pit 21 to the east of
the Emperor's tomb
Height: 10.2cm   Rim width: 0.6cm   Bore: 25cm
銅鉢　帝陵東側21号従葬坑から出土
口径25、高10.2、縁幅0.6cm

31. **陶漏壶** 帝陵东侧16号坑出土
直径10.1、高22.3、内径8.9厘米
Pottery dripping pot for measuring time unearthed from Pit 16 to the east
of the Emperor's tomb
Height: 22.3cm   Diameter: 10.1cm   Inner diameter: 8.9cm
陶漏壺（水時計）　帝陵東側16号従葬坑から出土
直径10.1、高22.3、内径8.9cm

33. **铜构件** 帝陵东侧16号坑出土　长4、宽2.5厘米
Bronze component unearthed from Pit 16 to the east of the Emperor's tomb
Width: 2.5cm   Length: 4cm
銅製の部材　帝陵東側16号従葬坑から出土　長4、幅2.5cm

34. **铁权** 帝陵东侧15号坑出土
最大径5.3~8.8、高3.2~5.5厘米
Iron weight unearthed from Pit 15 to the east of the Emperor's tomb
Height: 3.2~5.5cm   Diameter: 5.3~8.8cm
鉄権　帝陵東側15号従葬坑から出土
最大径5.3~8.8、高3.2~5.5cm

35. **铜弩机**
帝陵东侧13号坑出土　长7.5、高6厘米
Bronze cross-bow trigger unearthed from Pit 13 to the east
of the Emperor's tomb   Height: 6cm   Length: 7.5cm
銅弩　帝陵東側13号従葬坑から出土　高6、長7.5cm

36. 铜铺首　帝陵东侧13号坑出土　长8.3、宽6厘米
Bronze ornament unearthed from Pit 13 to the east of the
Emperor's tomb　Length: 8.3cm　Width: 6cm
銅鋪首　帝陵東側13号従葬坑から出土　長8.3、幅6cm

37. 玉璧　帝陵东侧18号坑出土　外径9.2、内径2.6厘米
Jade Bi unearthed from Pit 18 to the east of the Emperor's tomb
The outside diameter: 9.2cm　The inside diameter: 2.6cm
玉璧　帝陵東側18号従葬坑から出土
外径9.2、内径2.6cm

38. 铜构件　帝陵东侧16号坑出土　长12.5、宽3~5.8、厚2厘米
Bronze components unearthed from Pit 16 to the east of the Emperor's tomb
Width: 3-5.8cm　Length: 12.5cm　Thickness: 2cm
銅製の部材　帝陵東側16号従葬坑から出土　長12.5、幅3~5.8、厚2cm

39. 发掘前的帝陵南阙门遗址
Ruins of the South Gate of the Emperor's tomb
発掘前の帝陵南門闕遺跡

40. 帝陵南阙门遗址发掘现场
Excavation site of the ruins of the South Gate of the Emperor's tomb
帝陵南門闕遺跡の発掘現場

41. 帝陵南阙门遗址散水石及回廊

Pebble stones and the winding corridors at the western site of the South Gate

帝陵南門闕遺跡、散水石及び回廊

42. 帝陵南阙门遗址东阙台南回廊阶梯

Stairway of the southern winding corridor of the South Gate

帝陵南門闕東望台南回廊の版築階段

43. "千秋万岁" 瓦当
帝陵南阙门遗址出土　直径18厘米
Eaves tile with the inscription of "Long Live" unearthed from
the South Gate　Diameter: 18cm
"千秋万岁"瓦当　帝陵南門闕遺跡から出土　直径18cm

44. "与天无极" 瓦当
帝陵南阙门遗址出土　直径16、厚3厘米
Eaves tile with the inscription of "Lasting forever" unearthed
from the South Gate　Diameter: 16cm　Thickness: 3cm
"与天无极"瓦当　帝陵南門闕遺跡から出土
直径16　厚3cm

45. "长乐未央" 瓦当
帝陵南阙门遗址出土　直径16.3厘米
Eaves tile with the inscription of "Happy life"
unearthed from the South Gate
Diameter : 16.3cm
"長樂未央"瓦当
帝陵南門闕遺跡から
出土　直径16.3cm

46. "与天久长" 瓦当
帝陵南阙门遗址出土　直径17厘米
Eaves tile with the inscription of "Ever Lasting" unearthed from
the South Gate　Diameter: 17cm
"与天久长"瓦当　帝陵南門闕遺跡から出土　直径17cm

47. "永奉无疆" 瓦当
帝陵南阙门遗址出土　直径17.5厘米
Eaves tile with the inscription of "Longevity" unearthed from
the South Gate　Diameter: 17.5cm
"永奉无疆"瓦当　帝陵南門闕遺跡から出土　直径17.5cm

48. 帝陵南阙门遗址保护建筑
South Gate-tower Protection Hall
帝陵の南門闕遺跡

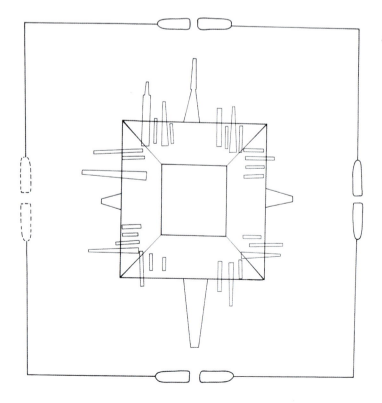

49. 后陵陵园钻探平面图
Plan map of the Empress' tomb
皇后陵園の試掘平面図

51. 帝陵陵园3号排水渠遗址
Ruins of the drainage system of
the Emperor's tomb
帝陵園の3号排水溝遺跡

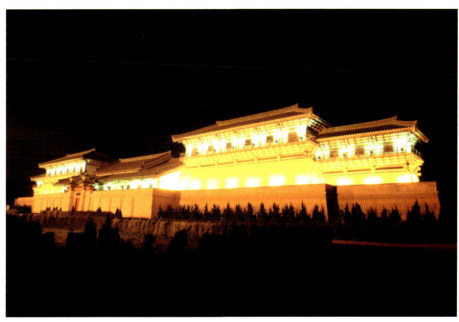

50. 帝陵南阙门遗址保护建筑夜景
Night scene of South Gate-tower Protection Hall
帝陵の南門闕遺跡

气势雄浑壮阔的汉阳陵

31

52. 帝陵外藏坑保护展示厅外景
Exterior scencery of the Protection Hall of Burial Pits
帝陵外藏坑保護展示ホールの外景

二、帝陵外藏坑保护展示厅

　　考古发掘资料表明，围绕帝陵封土的四周，有呈放射状分布的外藏坑81座。它们长短不一，内涵各异，充满着神秘色彩。1998年，经过对帝陵东侧北部10座外藏坑进行发掘清理，出土了各种陶俑、动物陶塑、生活用具、粮仓、兵器、车马器、玺印、封泥等珍贵文物数万件。从出土器物的内容、分布以及封泥、印章上的文字推测，这些外藏坑的设置很可能具有某种象征意义，代表着当时中央政府的不同官署和宫廷内设机构，是西汉时期宫廷文化真实而形象的再现。

　　为有效保护和合理利用这一重要考古发现，2006年3月在原址上建成帝陵外藏坑保护展示厅，它是博物苑最核心的一组建筑，建筑面积7856平方米，投资近1亿元。因建筑紧靠陵体一侧，为保护陵园原有历史和自然环境风貌，其设计为全地下的建筑，为全国首座现代化的地下遗址博物馆，构架起帝陵10个外藏坑的保护展示空间，地面则覆以草皮植被。它的内部设计融合了现代建筑理念和文物保护的科技手段，采用国际先进的文物保护专利技术，通过真空镀膜电加热玻璃幕墙和玻璃通道将游客与文物隔离，为观众与文物遗址分别创造两个不同的温湿度环境，在最大限度科学保护文物遗址的前提下，也给观众多角度欣赏和接近文物提供了条件。此外，博物苑中还采用先进的光成像技术，通过虚拟成像的手段再现了汉景帝时期的某些重大历史事件、重要历史人物，使得虚拟的历史人物和出土的文物实物有机地融合在一个特定的历史场景之中。该项目无论从建筑设计、文物保护技术、文物展示手段等各个方面看，都代表了国内遗址博物馆的先进水平，对于展示我国在古迹保护方面的最新成果具有积极的现实意义。

B. Protection Hall of Burial Pits

The archaeological discoveries have indicated that radiating from the burial mound of the emperor's tomb, there are 81 burial pits, which were built of different sizes and buried with various objects, full of mysterious coloring. In 1998, after excavation of ten such outside burial pits to the northeast of the emperor's tomb, those unearthed were thousands of valuable cultural relics such as all kinds of pottery figurines, pottery animals, daily utensils, granaries, weapons, horses and chariots, seals and lutes. Judged by the substance and location of the unearthed objects and the writings on the lutes and seals, we can conjecture that all the outside burial pits were built to have some symbolic meanings, representing some certain government bureaus and court agencies. They truly and vividly reproduce the court culture of the Western Han Dynasty.

In order to effectively preserve and properly utilize such an important archaeological discovery, an exhibition hall is built on March, 2006 on the site of the ten pits to form a group of core structures of the museum. It has a construction space of 7,856 square meters with a total investment of close to one hundred million RMB. Due to its location close to the burial mound, the exhibition hall is built underground so as to maintain the original historical and natural landscapes of the tomb area and thus, becomes the nation's first modern underground on-the-site museum to house the ten outside burial pits of the emperor's tomb for both preservation and exhibition. The surface is covered by the lawn. Its interior design combines the modern construction concepts with scientific methods for preserving cultural relics. The museum has adopted the internationally advanced patented technology to preserve cultural relics by using the electric-heating glass wall and glass passageway to separate the visitors from the cultural relics, so that the visitors and the cultural relics are placed into two different environments with different temperatures and humidity in order to provide the best possible condition to preserve the sites and the cultural relics, as well as the condition for the visitors to get close to and to appreciate the exhibits from different perspectives. In addition, the museum also employs sophisticated spectra vision technology to recreate some important historical events or important historical figures of the era of Emperor Jingdi. These invented historical figures are merged organically with the unearthed cultural relics in a certain historical scene. In terms of its structure design, preservation technology and displaying methods of the cultural relics, this project represents the advanced standard of domestic on-the-site museums and has great significance to demonstrate our country's latest achievements in preserving the ancient ruins.

2. 帝陵外蔵坑保護展示ホール

考古資料によって、帝陵封土の周りに８１座の外蔵坑が放射線のように分布していることが明らかになった。これらの外蔵坑は大きさがそれぞれ違い、神秘的な色彩を醸し出している。１９９８年、帝陵東側北部の１０座の外蔵坑を対象にして発掘作業が行われ、各種陶俑、生活用具、粮倉、兵器、車馬器、印、封泥など数万件の貴重な文物が出土した。出土した器物の種類、分布及び封泥、印章の文字などから、これら外蔵坑の設置が象徴的な意味を備え、当時の中央政府のそれぞれ異なった官署や宮廷機構を表わし、前漢時期における宮廷文化の形状が再現できる。

この重大な発見を有効に保護、利用するため、２００６年３月に遺跡をそのまま保護、展示できる帝陵外蔵坑保護展示ホールが建てられた。その展示ホールは漢陽陵博物苑の中心建築で、建築面積７８５６平方メートル、約１億元の資金が使用された。陵園の自然環境を保護するため、展示ホールは全て地下建築の様式を用いた全国で初めての現代的地下遺跡博物館であり、１０座の外蔵坑が地下に保護され、地上には芝生や植物が敷かれている。その内部のデザインは現代建築理念と文化財保護の科学的手段を一体化にし、真空コーティング電熱ガラススクリーンとガラス通路を使用することによって、観客と文物は隔離され、それぞれ温湿度の違う空間を創り出し、最大限の科学技術によって遺跡を保護する前提の下、多角度からのまたより近くからの文物鑑賞を提供できる。また、ヴァーチャル映像を利用し、漢の景帝時代に発生した重大事件やその時代の有名な人物も、この先進技術によって出土実物と共に歴史の情景を作り出す。つまり、国内遺跡博物館の中で漢陽陵帝陵外蔵坑保護展示ホールは、建築設計、展示方法、文化財保護技術などの面において先進的な水準を有し、古遺跡保護の最新成果を展示するという積極的な意義がある。

53. 西汉帝王世系公绍碑

The stone tablet of the genealogy of
the emperors of the Western Han Dynasty

前漢帝王家系碑

54. 帝陵外藏坑保护展示厅入口

Entrance of the Protection Hall of
Burial Pits

帝陵外葬坑保護展示ホールの入り口

55. 序言厅
Preface Hall.
序言ホール

56. 通入遗址区的斜坡通道与钢结构
Ramp and its steel structures leading to
the sites.
遺跡区に入る坂道と鋼組み立て

帝陵外藏坑保护展示厅

57. 被特殊玻璃合围封闭的遗址区和特殊照明
Sites and its special lighting sealed by the special glass.
特別ガラスに密封された遺跡区と特殊照明

58. 被特殊玻璃合围封闭的遗址区和特殊照明
Sites and its special lighting sealed by the special glass.
特別ガラスに密封された遺跡区と特殊照明

59. 被特殊玻璃合围封闭的遗址区和特殊照明
Sites and its special lighting sealed by the special glass.
特別ガラスに密封された遺跡区と特殊照明

60. 横跨在遗址区上的 U 形玻璃通道
U-shaped glass passageway over the site.
遺跡区の上にかかっている「U」字形ガラス通路

61. 横跨在遗址区上的 U 形玻璃通道
U-shaped glass passageway over the site.
遺跡区の上にかかっている「U」字形ガラス通路

62. 考古工作者在封闭的环境中
从事发掘清理
Archaeologists excavating in the sealed
environment.
密封環境の中で発掘作業をしてい
る考古学者

63. 考古工作者在封闭的环境中从事
发掘清理
Archaeologists excavating in the sealed
environment.
密封環境の中で発掘作業をしている考古
学者

64. 倒 L 形的 13 号坑玻璃封闭装置
Glass sealing unit of the inverted L-shaped
Pit 13.
逆「L」字形１３号坑のガラス密封装置

65. 倒 L 形的 13 号坑玻璃封闭装置
Glass sealing unit of the inverted L-shaped Pit 13.
逆「L」字形１３号坑のガラス密封装置

66 踩踏在玻璃地面上俯视坑内文物
Overlooking the cultural relics in the pit through the glass floor.
ガラス地面の上から坑内の文物を俯瞰している

67. 透过玻璃从侧面观赏出土文物
Viewing through the glass the unearthed cultural relics from the side.
ガラス越しに出土文物を観賞している

68. 透过玻璃从侧面观赏出土文物
Viewing through the glass the unearthed cultural relics from the side.
ガラス越しに出土文物を観賞している

69. 帝陵东侧14号外藏出土的盛放丝织物的顶漆木箱遗迹局部
Partial ruins of the lacquer box with silk clothes in Pit 14 to the east of Emperor's tomb
帝陵東側の14号外葬坑で発見したシルク織物を収める漆箱の痕跡

70. 14号坑内出土的珍禽异兽骨骼
The skeletons of rare birds and animals in Pit 14.
14号坑から出土した珍しい動物の骨

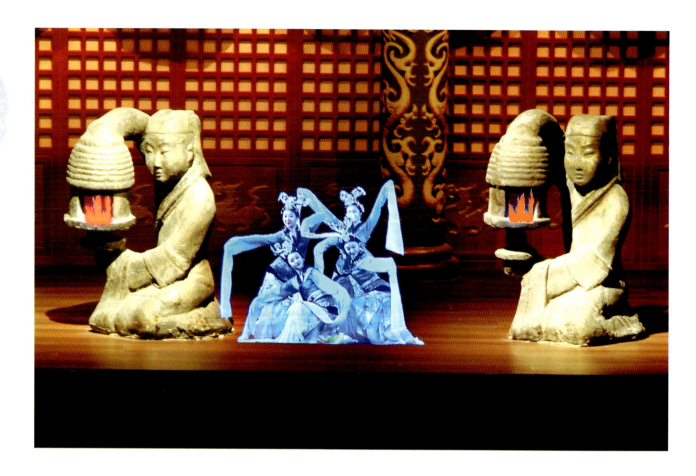

71. 幻影成像演示，再现西汉历史风云
   Demonstration of the spectra vision technology to create some important historical
   events and important historical figures of the western Han Dynasty
   映像デモンストレーションで再現した前漢の歴史

72. 12 号坑的复原陈列
Restored Pit 12.
12号坑の復元陳列

73. 充满神秘色彩的辅助陈列大厅
Auxiliary exhibition hall full of mysterious coloring.
神秘的な色彩を醸し出す補助陳列ホール

74. 密集陈列的汉代陶器
Densely exhibited Han pottery utensils.
密集陳列された漢代陶器

75～77. 专题陈列柜
Showcase of special subjects.
テーマ陳列ケース

78. 复原的汉代武士
Restored Han warrior.
復元された漢代武士

79. 复原的汉代舞女
Restored Han dancing girl.
復元された漢代舞女

80. 复原的汉代文吏
Restored Han official.
復元された漢代文吏

82. 汉阳陵考古陈列馆外景
Outdoor scene of the Han Yangling Archaeological Museum
漢陽陵考古陳列館外景

C. Han Yangling Archaeological Museum With Distinctive Features

Located on the southern side of the tombs of the Emperor and Empress, the Han Yangling Archaeological Museum was open to the public on September, 1999. In order to well maintain the entire historical style of the mausoleum, the museum was built semi-subterranean with two stories, covering an area of 3,750 square meters. It mainly displays 1,800 pieces/or groups, of all kinds of relics uncovered from the burial pits of the Emperor's tomb, southern burial pits, satellite tombs as well as from the sites of ritual buildings. All the exhibits are arranged with distinctive archaeological characteristics. Since its grand opening, the museum has attracted great attentions from all fields of the society and has received a lot of visitors including communist party and state leaders like Jiang Zemin, Li Peng, Li Ruihuan, Li Lanqing, Wei Jianxing, Li Tieying, Wu Guanzheng and some foreign government heads and officials. At present, the museum is the teaching base for the students and interns of the archaeological departments of many universities.

3．オリジナル漢陽陵考古陳列館

漢陽陵考古陳列館は帝陵と后陵の南側に位置しており、1999年9月正式に落成しオープンした。陵園全体の風格を保護するために、半地下式の建築様式をしている。建築面積は3750平方キロメートル。漢陽陵帝陵従葬坑、南区従葬坑、従葬墓園及び礼制建築遺跡から発掘された1800件（組）あまりの各種文物はここに陳列されている。陳列方法も考古学の特徴が鮮明であり、開館して以来、社会各階の注目を集めている。江沢民、李鵬、李瑞環、李嵐清、尉建行、李鉄映、呉官正など党と国の指導者たちも来館して視察した。たくさんの外国首脳と政治家たちも見物に来た。現在、ここは大学の歴史考古学の実習基地となっている。

83. 汉阳陵考古陈列馆序厅
Preliminary section of the archaeological museum
漢陽陵考古陳列館序ホール

84. 第一单元——阳陵概况介绍及礼制性建筑遗址出土文物
Unit One–The briefing of Han Yangling as well as the relics unearthed from the ruins of the ritual buildings
第一章——陽陵概況と礼制建築遺跡から出土された文物の展示

85. 第二单元——帝陵从葬坑出土文物陈列
Unit Two–Display of cultural relics unearthed from the burial pits
第二章——帝陵従葬坑から出土された文物の展示

86. 第五单元——陪葬墓园生活用具、兵器、车马器等各类文物陈列

Unit Five–Display of the daily necessities, weapons and ornaments of horses and chariots unearthed from the burial pits

第五章——従葬墓園の生活用具、兵器、車馬器などの展示

87. 第五单元——陪葬墓园M9K1马、牛、羊、猪、狗、鸡动物雕塑及男女侍从俑和生活用具等隧道式建筑结构复原陈列

Restoration of Pit 1 Tomb 9(satellite tomb) in which unearthed are pottery horses, oxen, sheep, goats, pigs, dogs and chickens as well as male and female servants and daily necessities

第五章——従葬墓園M9KI馬、牛、羊、豚、犬、鶏六種動物俑、男女侍従俑と生活用具などをトンネル式建築様式で復元して展示

88. 帝陵从葬坑地层叠压关系展示

Display of the layers of strata of the burial pits of the Emperor's tomb

帝陵従葬坑断面図

89. 1999 年 9 月 30 日汉阳陵考古陈列馆开馆剪彩仪式
Opening ceremony of the Han Yangling Archaeological Museum
on September 30, 1999
1999 年 9 月 30 日漢陽陵考古陳列館の開館セレモニー

90．二号建筑遗址外景
Scenery of No. 2 Architectural Site
二号建筑遗迹

四、陵园内的礼制性建筑遗址

陵园内以帝陵为中心，其布局四角拱围、左右对称、东西相连，形成了西汉时期帝王陵园的完整格局。陵园的核心区设有内外城，均为正方形，每边垣墙的中部设有阙门，阙门有左右对称的阙台。中间为门道，阙台由下到上有三层，由小到大有三出。内外城之间设有大型礼制性建筑遗址。 一号建筑遗址位于帝陵西南方向约 450 米处，遗址东西长 320 米，南北宽 210 米，外围有壕沟、垣墙，垣墙以内有保存较为完好的规模较大的建筑遗址。1992 年至 1993 年对东南部的 1000 平方米进行了试掘，清理出墙基、柱础、庭院等建筑遗迹，出土了大量的瓦当、铺地砖等建筑材料。值得一提的是在一段数十米长的南北向墙基下出土了 230 余件塑衣式粉彩陶俑和部分动物俑，有舞女俑，也有奏乐俑，成为一组伎乐场面。 二号建筑遗址（又称罗经石建筑遗址）位于帝陵东南方向约 300 米处，平面为正方形，边长 260 米，可分为内外两层建筑。外围有壕沟，沟内的四角有曲尺形廊房，四边的中部各有一门道，门道内侧各有两孔渗水井。内有中心建筑一座，平面为正方形，边长 53.7 米。遗址内高外低，中心高于周围地面 5.3 米，夯筑而成。遗址的中部有一中心柱石，外围有砖铺回廊和散水，每边有 14 个壁柱和三处门道。门道的台阶上铺有四神纹空心砖。四面的铺地砖、墙壁、屋面上按东、南、西、北方位分别涂有青、红、白、黑四种颜色。遗址布局规整，气势宏伟，是西汉时期的大型礼制建筑。

D. Remains of the Ritual Architectures in the Yangling Mausoleum

With the Emperor's Mausoleum in the center, the graveyard was once surrounded by walls on four sides. It is a representative Western Han Dynasty mausoleum for its symmetry and consistency. Square shaped inner and outer city walls were built in the epicenter of the cemetery, each wall has a side tower in the middle. Two side terraces with a pylon between them were built on both sides of every tower. The terrace has three layers from little to large. There are many remains of the big-scaled ritual architectures between the two city walls. Among them are No. 1 and No. 2 architectural remains.

No.1 Architectural Site is located about 450 meters to the southwest of the emperor's mausoleum. It is 320 meters long from east to west and 210 meters wide from south to north. Within the entrenchment and city wall, large-scaled architectural remains preserved quite well were discovered. Trial excavations were conducted in an area of 1000 square meters in its south-west from 1992 to 1993. Architectural remains such as wall bases, plinths and courtyards were unearthed, and a large number of tiles and bricks for paving floors were also discovered. More than 230 painted pottery figurines with molded clothes and some animal figures were unearthed underneath a south-north oriented wall of dozens of meters. The figurines include dancers and musicians, thus forming a scene of entertainment.

No. 2 Architectural Site, also named the Luojing Stone Architectural Remains, is located about 300 meters to the southeast of the emperor's mausoleum. It is in square shape and each side is 260 meters in length. The buildings can be classified as inner and outer ones. The entrenchment outside has L-shaped porches at each corner. A pylon was found in the middle of every wall, each side of it has two wells. A main square-shaped building was within the walls, with each side 53.7 meters. The area within the walls is 5.3 meters higher than its coterminous area. It was once rammed. A stone pillar was discovered in the center of the remains. Brick-paved corridor and aprons surround the pillar, with 14 columns along the walls and 3 pylons on each side. The steps of the pylons were paved with hollow bricks with the pattern of four gods. The bricks, walls and rooftops were painted blue, red, white and black respectively corresponding to the four directions of east, south, west and north. The neat layout and magnificent vigor made it a large-scaled ritual complex in the Western Han Dynasty.

4. 前陵園内の礼制建築遺跡

陵園全体は帝陵を中心とし、建築物は4隅を取り囲み、南北は対称して、東西に繋がっている。前漢時代の独特の皇帝陵園の配置を形成した。陵園の中心部に内外城が設けられ、正方形をなし、4辺の壁それぞれの中心には門がある。門の下から上まで3層あり、下から上に次第に大きくなる"三出"と呼ばれる台がある。城の外とうちの間には大型礼制性建築遺跡が多数あり、そのうち、一号、二号遺跡が一番重要である。一号建築遺跡は帝陵西南約450メートルの場所に位置する。東西には320メートルあり、南北には210メートルある。外側に壕溝が巡り、土壁の中に状態よく保存された建築遺跡がある。1992年から1993年まで、東南部1000平方メートルを試掘し、壁土台、柱台、庭などの遺跡が発見され、大量の瓦やレンガなど建築材料が出土された。特に、230件あまりの塑衣式粉彩陶俑と動物俑が出土され、そのうちの歌舞俑、伎楽俑から当時の伎楽の場面が推測できる。二号遺跡（羅経石遺跡とも言う）は帝陵東南約300メートルの場所に位置しており、幅260メートルの正方形で、外側に壕溝が巡っている。、溝の内側四つの角に廊屋がある。溝四つの壁の真ん中にそれぞれ門道があり、その内側に2つの排水井戸が設けられている。遺跡中部から地面より5.3メートルの所に版築の幅53.7平方メートルの正方形土台が発見され、主体建築の土台だと思われる。この土台の中心には石柱がある。土台の回りはレンガが敷かれている回廊と散水があり、四つの面にそれぞれ14の壁柱と3つの門がある。門の階段に四神紋様の空心レンガが敷かれている。四面のレンガ、壁、屋根は東南西北の方位によって、青、赤、白、黒四種類の色に染められている。この建築遺跡の配置は整っており、規模は非常に大きく、前漢時代の重要な礼制建築であると思われる。

91. 二号建筑遗址及帝陵全景
Panorama of No. 2 Architectural Site and Emperor's tomb
二号建築遺跡及び帝陵全景

92. 正在发掘中的二号建筑遗址中心部分鸟瞰
A bird view over the ruins of No. 2 Architectural Site in excavation
発掘している二号建築遺跡

93~95. 二号建筑遗址保护与展示现场
The display of the ruins of No. 2 Architectural Site
二号建築遺構の保護展示現場

96. 玉璧　二号建筑遗址出土　直径4.8、3.7厘米
　　Jade Bi, burial object, unearthed from the ruins of No. 2 Architectural Site　Diameter: 4.8, 3.7 cm
　　玉璧　二号建築遺跡出土　直径4.8、3.7cm

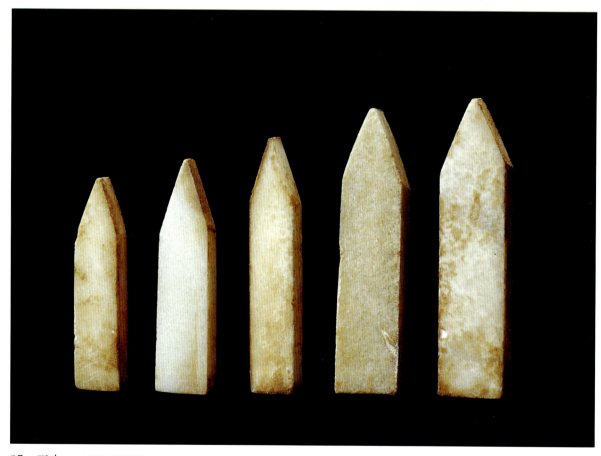

97. 玉圭　二号建筑遗址出土　长6.8、7.4、8.1、9、9.3　宽1.7、1.9、1.6、2.1、2.2厘米
　　A set of Jade Gui, burial objects, unearthed from the ruins of No. 2 Architectural Site
　　Length: 6.8,7.4,8.1,9.3cm　Width: 1.7,1.9,1.6,2.1,2.2 cm
　　一組の玉圭　二号建築遺跡出土　長6.8、7.4、8.1、9、9.3　幅1.7、1.9、1.6、2.1、2.2cm

98. 陶质六博　二号建筑遗址出土　边长 34.5 厘米
Pottery chessboard unearthed from the ruins of No. 2 Architectural Site　Length: 34.5 cm
陶製六博　二号建築遺跡出土　辺長 34.5cm

99. 青龙纹空心砖　二号遗址出土　残长 66、宽 37 厘米
Hollow brick with dragon designs unearthed from the ruins of No. 2 Architectural Site
Remain length: 66cm　Width: 37cm
青龍紋空心レンガ　二号建築遺跡出土　残長 66、幅 37cm

100. 玄武纹空心砖
二号遗址出土
残长 52、宽 34、厚 10 厘米
Hollow brick with turtle and snake design
unearthed from the ruins of No. 2 Architectural Site
Remain length: 52cm
Width: 34cm　Thickness: 10cm
玄武紋空心レンガ　二号建築遺跡出土残
残長 52、幅 34、厚 10cm

五、排列有序的南北区从葬坑

　　南北区从葬坑分别位于帝陵的东南和西北方向450米处，均占地96000平方米，各有对称分布的从葬坑24座。最长的坑299米、最短的坑25.2米，坑宽一般3.5米左右，最宽者10米，坑深一般7～8米、坑间距20米左右。从葬坑均为竖穴土圹地下隧道式建筑。1990年5月至1999年9月通过对南区5座从葬坑的局部试掘和对10座从葬坑的全面发掘，出土著衣式彩绘陶俑及兵器、车马器、生产工具、生活用具等各类文物30000余件。从排列阵容和出土文物来看属于军事性质，可能是西汉时期南军和北军的缩影。

101. 南区 20 号从葬坑发掘现场
Excavation site of No.20 burial pit in the
southern area of the Mausoleum
南区 20 号従葬坑の発掘現場

E.Regularly Arranged Burial Pits in Southern and Northern Areas

The burial pits of southern and northern areas are located respectively 450m away to the southeast and northeast of the Emperor's tomb, each covering an area of 96,000 square meters. There are 24 burial pits in each area with the longest pit being 299m and the shortest 25.2m. The pits average 3.5m in width, yet, the widest pit is 10m. They are 7m to 8m in depth and there is a space of 20m between each pit. All the burial pits were built to be vertically tunnel-like subterraneans. From the May of 1990 to the September of 1999, in the southern area of Han Yangling, 10 burial pits were fully excavated and 5 pits were partially excavated. The excavation of these pits have yielded 30,000 pieces of cultural relics including clothed and painted pottery figurines as well as weapons, ornaments of horses and chariots, tools, daily necessities. Based on the fact that the formations and the unearthed relics are of military nature, therefore, these burial pits are very likely to symbolize the Southern and the Northern Army of the Western Han Dynasty.

5．配置整う南、北区従葬坑

南、北区従葬坑はそれぞれ帝陵の東南と西北450mのところに位置しており、各96000㎡の面積を占め、対称分布の従葬坑が24条配列される。最長の坑は299mで、最短の坑は25.2mである。坑の幅は大体3.5mで、一番幅広い坑は10mを超える。坑の深さは7－8m、坑の間隔は20mぐらいである。従葬坑は全部竪穴式地下トンネルのような建築様式になっている。1990年5月から1999年9月まで南区従葬坑5棟を一部分試掘し、10棟を全体発掘し、着衣式彩絵陶俑、兵器、車馬器、生産工具、生活用具などの文物が30000件余り出土された。配列の並びと出土した文物から見ると、軍事的なものであることが分かり、前漢時期の"南軍"と"北軍"と推定できる。

102～104. 南区 20 号从葬坑南半部铠
        甲武士俑群

A group of armored warriors in the
southern part of No. 20 burial pit in
the southern area of the Mausoleum
南区 20 号従葬坑の発掘現場南
半部甲冑武士俑群

105. 南区 10 号从葬坑发掘现场
Excavation site of No. 10 burial pit in the southern area of the Mausoleum
南区 10 号従葬坑の発掘現場

106. 南区 10 号从葬坑武士俑群局部
Part of the warriors in Pit 10 in the southern area
南区 10 号従葬坑の武士俑群

107. 南区 17 号从葬坑发掘现场
Excavation site of No.17 burial pit
in the southern area of the
Mausoleum
南区 17 号従葬坑の発掘現場

108. 南区 20 号从葬坑朱红色屏风遗迹及武士陶俑
Remains of the red screens as well as the pottery warriors in
No.20 burial pit in the southern area of the Mausoleum
南区 20 号従葬坑の朱色屏風遺跡と武士陶俑

109. 南区 5 号从葬坑出土的朱红色屏风遗迹及执铍武士俑
Remains of the red screens as well as the warriors holding long spears in
No. 5 burial pit in the southern area of the Mausoleum
南区 5 号従葬坑の朱色屏風遺跡とよろいをつけた武士俑

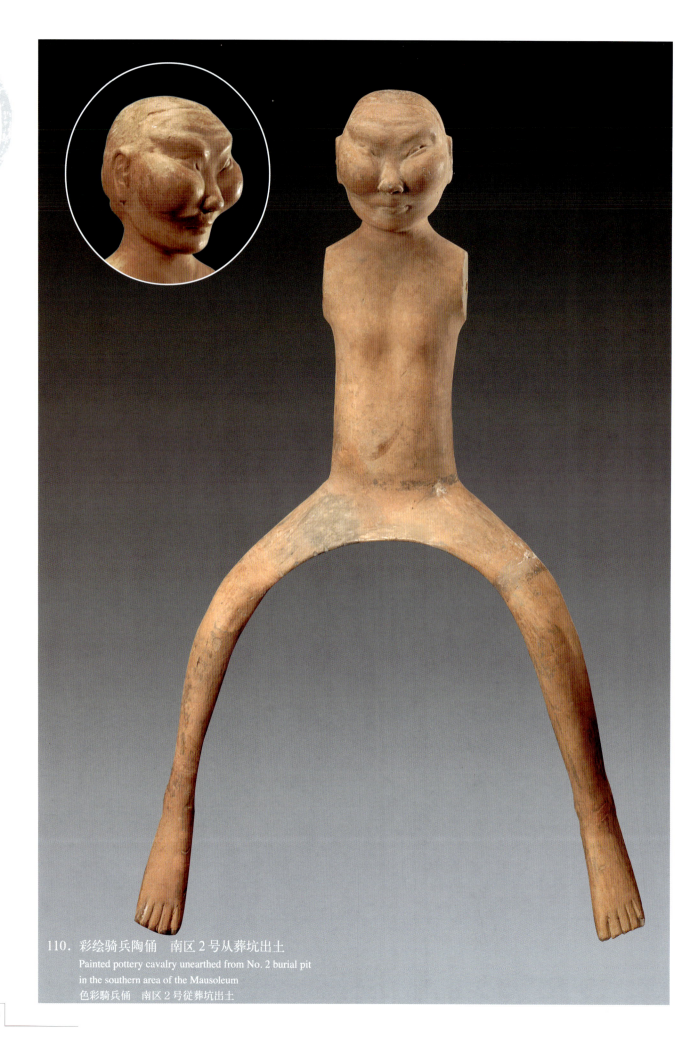

110. 彩绘骑兵陶俑　南区 2 号从葬坑出土
Painted pottery cavalry unearthed from No. 2 burial pit
in the southern area of the Mausoleum
色彩骑兵俑　南区 2 号従葬坑出土

111. 著衣式铠甲武士陶俑　高56.5厘米
Armored warrior　Height: 56.5cm
著衣式鎧をつけた武士俑　高56.5cm

112. 著衣式铠甲武士陶俑　高57.5厘米
Armored pottery warrior　Height: 57.5cm
着衣式鎧をつけた武士俑　高57.5cm

113. 著衣式铠甲武士步行陶俑
高 53 厘米
Armored pottery warrior in a walking
position   Height: 53cm
着衣式鎧をつけた行走俑   高 53cm

114. 著衣式裸体武士陶俑 高 57~62 厘米
Pottery warrior Height: 57~62cm
着衣式武士陶俑組 高 57~62cm

115. 著衣式步行武士陶俑　高 55 厘米
Walking pottery warrior originally dressed up
Height: 55cm
着衣式行走武士俑　高 55cm

116. 形态各异的著衣式彩绘武士陶俑头
Various features of the painted warriors
着衣式色彩武士俑头部

117. 118. 扎陌额、戴武弁著衣式彩绘武士陶俑头及后部　残高 10 厘米
Warrior's head showing the traces of headband and hat
Remain height: 10cm
"陌额"をかぶり、"武弁"をつける武士俑頭部　残高 10cm

119. 铜质攻城破门器鱼尾形铜镦
南区从葬坑出土　长 33、宽 11.8、外径 7.0 厘米
Bronze battering-ram with fish tail design unearthed from
a burial pit in the southern area
Length: 33cm　Width: 11.8cm　Outside diameter: 7.0cm
魚尾型銅镦 南区従葬坑出土
長 33 、幅 11.8、外径 7.0cm

120. 铜质攻城破门器前峰
南区从葬坑出土　长 23.2、宽 15.2、高 13.1 厘米
The front blade of battering-ram unearthed from a burial
pit in the southern area
Length: 23.2cm　Width: 15.2cm　Height: 13.1cm
城壁の門を突く道具　南区従葬坑出土
長 23.2 、幅 15.2、高 13.1cm

121. 铜钺　南区从葬坑出土　高 7.9、宽 11.3 厘米
Bronze Yue (a small ax) unearthed from a burial
pit in the southern area
Height: 7.9cm　Width: 11.3cm
銅钺　南区従葬坑出土　高 7.9 、幅 11.3cm

122. 铜铙
南区从葬坑出土 高 12.1、宽 6 × 4.1 厘米
Bronze Nao (a musical instrument) unearthed from a burial
pit in the southern area
Width: 6 × 4.1cm　Height: 12.1cm
銅铙　南区従葬坑出土　長 12.1、幅 6 × 4.1cm

123. 柳叶形铁矛头　南区从葬坑出土　长17.2厘米
Four-edged iron spears unearthed from a burial pit in the southern area
Length: 17.2cm
柳葉っぱ型鉄製の矛先　南区従葬坑出土　長17.2cm

124. 铁剑　南区从葬坑出土　长37.6、36.2、34.4厘米
Iron swords unearthed from a burial pit in the southern area
Length: 37.6cm　36.2cm　34.4cm
鉄剣　南区従葬坑出土　長37.6、36.2、34.4cm

125. 铜镞　南区从葬坑出土　长3.6厘米
Bronze arrows unearthed from a burial pit in the southern area
Length: 3.6cm
銅鏃　南区従葬坑出土　長3.6cm

126. 卜字形铁戟
南区从葬坑出土　长4.8、扁体宽0.8厘米
Iron halberd unearthed from a burial pit in the southern area
Length: 4.8cm　Width: 0.8cm
"卜"字型鉄戟　南区従葬坑出土　長4.8、平均幅0.8cm

127. 旗杆顶端铜饰
南区2号从葬坑出土　长4厘米
Copper ornamental caps on top of posts unearthed from
No.2 burial pit in the southern area
Length: 4cm
銅飾　南区2号従葬坑出土　長4cm

128. 陶炉台
南区20号从葬坑出土
长43.4、高22.8、宽23.2厘米
Pottery furnace unearthed from No. 20 burial pit in the southern area
Length: 43.4cm　Width: 23.2cm　Height: 22.8cm
陶製釜戸　南区20号従葬坑出土
長43.4　高22.8幅　23.2cm

129. 龟钮"车骑将军"金印
南区2号从葬坑出土
边长0.7、高0.6厘米
Tortoise- shaped gold seal bearing the inscripotions
"Cavalry Commander" unearthed from No.2 burial
pit in the southern area
Side length: 0.7cm　Height: 0.6cm
"車騎将軍"亀钮金印
南区2号従葬坑出土
边长0.7、高0.6cm

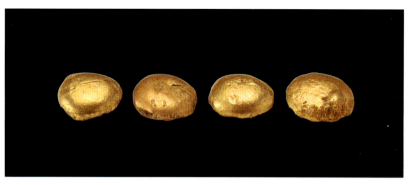

130. 金饼　南区 21 号从葬坑出土　直径 1.4、厚 0.32 厘米
Golden pieces unearthed from No. 21 burial pit in the southern area
Diameter: 1.4cm　Thickness: 0.32cm
金餅　南区 21 号従葬坑出土　直径 1.4、厚 0.32cm

131. 铜砝码　南区 21 号从葬坑出土
边长 0.6 × 0.7、高 0.5 厘米
A set of copper weights unearthed from
No. 21 burial pit in the southern area
Side length: 0.6 x 0.7cm　Height: 0.5cm
銅製分銅　南区 21 号従葬坑出土
边长 0.6 x 0.7、高 0.5cm

132. 鎏金铜轭帽　南区 6 号从葬坑出土
长 7 × 4、厚 2 厘米
Gold-plated yoke unearthed from No. 21
burial pit in the southern area
Length: 7 x 4cm　Thickness: 2cm
金銅製くびき　南区 6 号従葬坑出土
长 7 x 4、厚 2cm

汉阳陵博物馆

133. 铜斗　南区从葬坑出土
高8.7、口径11.3厘米
Copper Dou(a measurement of volume) unearthed from
a burial pit in the southern area
Height: 8.7cm　Bore:11.3cm
銅斗　南区従葬坑出土　高8.7、口径11.3cm

134. 铜升　南区从葬坑出土　高3.4、2.7、2.4、1.6　口径5.9、4.7、4.2、2.8厘米
Boronze Sheng (a unit of dry measure for grain) unearthed from a burial pit in the southern area
Height: 3.4,2.7,2.4,1.6cm　Bore:5.9,4.7,4.2,2.8cm
銅製量器　南区従葬坑出土　高3.4、2.7、2.4、1.6　口径5.9、4.7、4.2、2.8cm

135. 铜鉴　南区从葬坑出土
高3.6、口径6.1厘米
Bronze cooking vessel unearthed from a burial pit in the
southern area　Bore: 6.1cm　Height: 3.6cm
銅鑑　南区従葬坑出土　高3.6、口径6.1cm

136. 铜鍪　南区从葬坑出土
口径4.7、高6.6、腹径7.2厘米
Bronze cooking vessel unearthed from a burial pit in the
southern area
Bore: 4.7cm　Height: 6.6cm　Diameter: 7.2cm
銅鍪　南区従葬坑出土　高6.6、口径4.7、腹径7.2cm

137. 铜权　南区从葬坑出土　直径1.3、2、2.9　高0.7、1.2、1.7厘米
A set of bronze weight unearthed from a burial pit in the southern area
Diameter: 1.3, 2, 2.9cm　Height: 0.7, 1.2, 1.7cm
銅権　南区従葬坑出土　直径1.3、2、2.9　高0.7、1.2、1.7cm

138. 铜带钩　南区从葬坑出土　长1.5厘米
Bronze belt hooks unearthed from a burial pit in the southern area
Length: 1.5cm
銅製帯鈎　南区従葬坑出土　長1.5cm

139. 陶灶　南区从葬坑出土　通高21.5、长39、宽21.4、烟囱高8.5厘米
Pottery furnace unearthed from a burial pit in the southern area
Height: 21.5cm　Length: 39cm　Width: 21.4cm
Height of the chimney: 8.5cm
陶製釜戸の模型　南区従葬坑出土　通高21.5、長39、幅21.4、煙突高8.5cm

140. 陶井　南区从葬坑出土
　　　通高 17 厘米
　　　内径 19 厘米
　　　沿长 21 厘米
　　　Pottery well unearthed from a burial
　　　pit in the southern area
　　　Height: 17cm　Inner diameter: 19cm
　　　Length of the board side: 21cm
　　　陶製井戸の模型　南区従葬坑出土
　　　通高 17、内径 19、边長 21cm

141. 铜滑轮　南区从葬坑出土　长 30.6 厘米
　　　Bronze pulley unearthed from a burial pit in the southern area
　　　Length: 30.6cm
　　　銅滑車　南区従葬坑出土　長 30.6cm

143. 铁锯、铁凿、铁锸、铁锛　南区从葬坑出土
　　　长 10、6.2、4.1、2.8 厘米
　　　宽 1.8、1、2.4、2.4 厘米
　　　Iron saw　Length: 10cm　Width: 1.8cm
　　　Iron chisel　Length:6.2cm　Width: 1cm
　　　Iron spade　Length: 4.1　Width: 2.4cm
　　　Iron axe　Length: 2.8cm　Width: 2.4cm
　　　All unearthed from burial pits in the southern area
　　　铁锯、铁凿、铁锸、铁锛　南区従葬坑出土
　　　长 10、6.2、4.1、2.8cm　幅 1.8、1、2.4、2.4cm

142. 铁犁铧　南区从葬坑出土
　　　口宽 17.5 厘米、刃宽 3.8～5 厘米
　　　Iron ploughshare unearthed from a burial pit in the
　　　southern area
　　　Width: 17.5cm　Width of blade: 3.8-5cm
　　　鉄製すきの刃　南区従葬坑出土
　　　口幅 17.5、刃幅 3.8～5cm

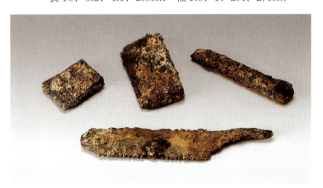

六、贵族陪葬墓园

阳陵陵园内有两处陪葬墓园，分别在北部和东部。北部的陪葬墓园在帝陵以北约600米处，现存两座陪葬墓，均为东西向中字型大墓，有封土，外围各有12座从葬坑。以墓室为中心，外围有边长170米的正方形围沟将墓园兆域划分清楚。东区的陪葬墓园位于东司马门外约100米以东。在东西长2500米、南北宽1500米的范围内，分布着200余个大小不等、年代早晚不同的贵族陪葬墓园。初步探明有不同时期的墓葬10000余座，已发掘2000余座，出土文物万余件，是目前已经探明的国内最大、最为完整的西汉时期的贵族陪葬墓园。

144. 汉阳陵陪葬墓园钻探平面图
Excavation map of Satellite Tombs
漢陽陵陪葬墓園試掘平面図

F. Satellite Tombs of the Nobles

There are two areas of satellite tombs in the Yangling Mausoleum. They are located in the north and east respectively. The one in the north is about 600 meters away from the emperor's mausoleum. It has two satellite tombs; both are huge ones by facing east and west in the shape of "zhong". They also have soil mounds; each one has 12 satellite pits. A square-shaped entrenchment, each side measuring 170 meters long, separates the two areas of satellite tombs. The one in the east is located about 100 meters outside of the Eastern Sima Gate. Within an area of 2,500meters long and 1,500 meters wide there are more than 200 cemeteries of nobles in different sizes and time. The initial excavation has revealed that there are over 10,000 tombs of different periods. About 2,000 have been excavated and more than 10,000 cultural relics have been unearthed. It is the biggest and most complete satellite tombs of the nobles in the Western Han Dynasty.

6. 貴族陪葬墓園

陽陵陵園内の北部と東部に2ヶ所の陪葬墓園がある。北部の陪葬墓園区には二つの陪葬がある。帝陵北部約600メートルの場所に位置し、中字型をなして東向きの封土付き陪塚となっている。外側には12個の従葬坑がある。墓室を中心とし、幅170メートルの正方形壕溝で墓園区域は分けられている。東部の陪葬墓園区は東司馬道の外側約100メートルの所にある。東西の幅は2500メートルで、南北の幅は1500メートルである。この範囲内に、200個余りの大きさと年代の違う貴族の陪塚が散在している。発掘調査を行ったお墓は約10000基で、全体発掘されたお墓は約2000基あり、合わせて各種類文物が一万件余り出土し、今まで分かっている前漢時代最も大きく、完全に揃っている貴族陪葬墓園である。

145. 陪葬墓园 M9K1 东区出土的动物俑
Pottery animals in the eastern part of the satellite tombs (Pit1 Tomb9)
M9K1 東区動物従葬坑の発掘現場

146. 陪葬墓园 M9K1 西区出土的各类彩绘陶器
Painted pottery in the western part of the satellite tombs (Pit1 Tomb9)
M9K1 西区から出土された各種彩色陶器

147. 陪葬墓园 M 85 发掘现场
Excavation site of No.85 satellite tomb
陪葬墓園 M85 発掘現場

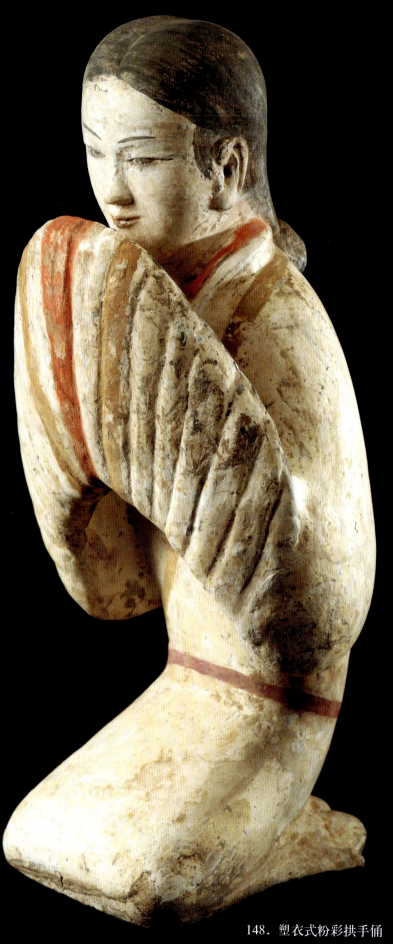

148. 塑衣式粉彩拱手俑　陪葬墓园 M130 周应墓出土　高 33 厘米
Painted pottery figurine folding her hands in a bow unearthed from Zhouying's
Tomb　Height: 33cm
塑衣式粉彩拱手俑　M130 周应墓出土　高 33cm

149. 塑衣式持物紫服跽坐俑　陪葬墓园周应墓出土　高41厘米
Painted squatting pottery figurine with violet molded clothes and holding an object
in hand unearthed from Zhouying's Tomb　Height: 41cm
塑衣式持物紫服跽座　周応墓出土　高41cm

150～152、塑衣式粉彩女立俑

陪葬墓园周应墓出土　高63厘米

Painted standing female figurine with molded clothes unearthed
from Zhouying's Tomb　Height: 63cm

塑衣式跽座粉彩女立俑　周应墓出土　高63cm

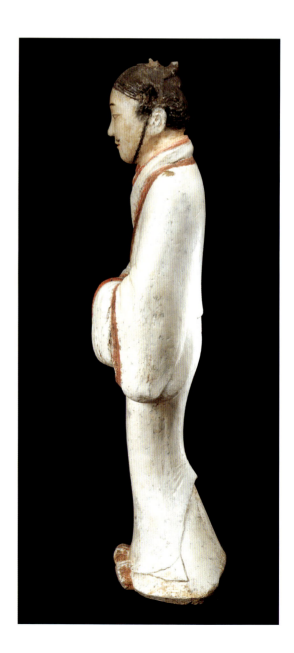

汉阳陵博物馆

153～155. 塑衣式粉彩文吏俑 陪葬墓园周应墓出土
Painted civil official figurine with molded clothes unearthed from
Zhouying's Tomb
塑衣式粉彩文官俑 周应墓出土

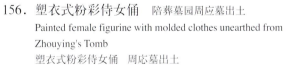

156. 塑衣式粉彩侍女俑　陪葬墓园周应墓出土
Painted female figurine with molded clothes unearthed from
Zhouying's Tomb
塑衣式粉彩侍女俑　周应墓出土

157. 塑衣式粉彩侍女俑　陪葬墓园周应墓出土
Painted female figurine with molded clothes unearthed from
Zhouying's Tomb
塑衣式粉彩侍女俑　周应墓出土

158. 著衣式彩绘侍女俑　陪葬墓园 M9K1 出土　高 53 厘米
Painted maids unearthed from the satellite tomb　Height: 53cm
着衣式彩色侍女俑　陪塚墓園 M9K1 出土　高 53cm

160. 著衣式彩绘牧童男俑
陪葬墓园 M9K1 出土
高 52.3 厘米
Painted pottery figurine unearthed
from the satellite tomb
Height: 52.3cm
著衣式彩色男牧童俑
陪塚墓園 M9K1 出土
高 52.3cm

159. 著衣式彩绘侍从男俑　陪葬墓园 M9K1 出土　高 57 厘米
Painted pottery figurine unearthed from the satellite tomb　Height: 57cm

著衣式彩色男侍従俑　陪塚墓園 M9K1 出土　高 57cm

161～162. 彩绘陶牛　陪葬墓园 M 9 K 1 出土　高 39、长 71、背宽 24.2 厘米
Painted pottery ox unearthed from the satellite tomb
Height: 39cm　Length: 71cm　Width of its back: 24.2cm
彩色陶牛　M9K1 東区動物從葬坑出土　高 39、長 71、背幅 24.2cm

163. 彩绘陶马　陪葬墓园M 9 K 1 出土　高59、长69厘米
Painted pottery horse unearthed from the satellite tomb
Height: 59cm　Length: 69cm
彩色陶馬　M9K1 東区動物従葬坑出土　高59、長69cm

164～165. 彩绘陶鱼　陪葬墓园出土
Painted pottery fish unearthed from the satellite tomb
彩色陶魚　陪塚出土

166. 彩绘陶鸡　陪葬墓园M 9 K 1 出土
公鸡：高14.8、长16.3厘米
母鸡：高11、长15厘米
Painted pottery chicken unearthed from the
satellite tomb
Rooster Height: 14.8cm　Length: 16.3cm
Hen Height: 11cm　Length: 15cm
彩色陶鶏　M9K1 東区動物従葬坑出十
雄：高14.8、長16.3cm
雌：高11、長15cm

167、168. "般邑家"铜锺

陪葬墓园出土　高43.7、口径6.2、腹径34、底径29.6厘米
Bronze bell belonging to the house of Ban unearthed from the satellite tomb
Height: 43.7cm　Bore: 6.2cm　Belly diameter: 34cm
Bottom diameter: 29.6cm
"般邑家"铜鐘　陪塚出土　高43.7
口径6.2　腹径34　底径29.6cm

169. "般邑家" 铜钫　陪葬墓园出土　高 31.7、口边长 9.7、底径 12.7 厘米

Bronze pot belonging to the house of Ban unearthed from the satellite tomb

Height: 31.7cm　Bore: 9.7cm　Bottom diameter: 12.7cm

"般邑家" 銅钫　陪塚出土　高 31.7、口边長 9.7、底径 12.7cm

汉阳陵博物馆

170. 铜熏炉　陪葬墓园出土　底径20.6、高15.4厘米
Bronze incense burner unearthed from the satellite tomb
Bottom diameter: 20.6cm　Height: 15.4cm
銅薰炉　陪塚出土　高15.4　底径20.6cm

171. 铜灯　陪葬墓园出土　高7.2、口径6.3、底径5.4厘米
Bronze lamp unearthed from the satellite tomb
Height: 7.2cm　Bore: 6.3cm　Bottom diameter: 5.4cm
銅灯　陪塚出土　高7.2　口径6.3　底径5.4cm

172. 铜豆　陪葬墓园出土　高11.3、口径9.2厘米
Bronze container unearthed from the satellite tomb
Height:11.3cm　Bore: 9.2cm
銅豆　陪塚出土　高11.3　口径9.2cm

173. 铜匜　陪葬墓园出土　通长37.4、高11.3厘米
Bronze basin unearthed from the satellite tomb
Length: 37.4cm　Height:11.3cm
銅匜　陪塚出土　通長37.4、高11.3cm

106

174. 铜盆及局部　陪葬墓园出土　高11.7、口径26.6厘米
Bronze basin and its part unearthed from the satellite tomb
Height: 11.7cm　Bore: 26.6cm
铜盆　陪塚出土　高11.7、口径26.6cm

175. 铜钵　陪葬墓园出土　通高14.1厘米
Bronze vessel unearthed from the satellite tomb
Height: 14.1cm
铜钵　陪塚出土　通高14.1cm

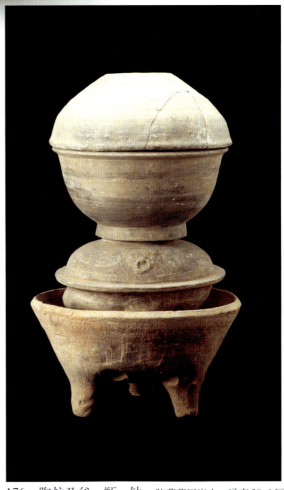

176. 陶炉及釜、甑、钵　陪葬墓园出土　通高38.6厘米
Pottery stove and cooking vessel unearthed from the satellite tomb　Height: 38.6cm
陶釜户　陪塚出土　通高38.6cm

177. 铁质炭火炉　陪葬墓园出土
高 11.5、长 32、宽 21 厘米
Iron charcoal stove unearthed from
the satellite tomb
Height: 11.5cm　Length: 32cm
Width: 21cm
鉄質火炉　陪塚出土
高 11.5　長 32　幅 21cm

178. 浮雕螭虎纹玉剑格　陪葬墓园出土　长 4.9、宽 1.7、厚 2.1 厘米
Jade scabbard with tiger design unearthed from the satellite tomb
Length: 4.9cm　Width: 1.7cm　Thickness: 2.1cm
虎紋浮彫剣形玉具　陪塚出土　長 4.9、幅 1.7、厚 2.1cm

179. 玉蝉　陪葬墓园出土　长 5、宽 2.6 厘米
Jade cicada unearthed from the satellite tomb
Length: 5cm　Width: 2.6cm
玉蝉　陪塚出土　長 5、幅 2.6cm

180. 白玉印坯
陪葬墓园出土
边长 1.4、高 1.1 厘米
White jade seal unearthed from the satellite tomb
Length of its side: 1.4cm　Height: 1.1cm
白玉印玉料　陪塚出土　边長 1.4、高 1.1cm

181. 漆盒遗迹　陪葬墓园出土
Remains of a lacqer box unearthed
from the satellite tomb
漆箱の跡　陪塚出土

182. 彩绘陶鼎　陪葬墓园出土　通高14.5、最宽处23.6厘米
Painted pottery tripod unearthed from the satellite tomb
Height: 14.5cm　Widest part: 23.6cm
彩色陶鼎　陪塚出土　通高14.5、最大幅23.6cm

183. 四坡房屋形陶仓　陪葬墓园M85出土　高50、宽33×55.5厘米
Pottery barn in the shape of a house unearthed from the satellite tomb
Height: 50cm　Width: 33 x 55.5cm
屋型陶倉　陪塚M85出土　高50、幅33×55.5cm

184. 陶魁　陪葬墓园出土
长 20、高 8、口宽 16.2 × 12.5 厘米
Pottery vessel unearthed from the satellite tomb
Length: 20cm　Height: 8cm　Bore: 16.2 x 12.5cm
陶魁　陪塚出土　长 20、高 8、口幅 16.2 × 12.5cm

185. 素面方形陶仓
陪葬墓园 M 85 出土
高 47.5、宽 55.6 × 33 厘米
Pottery barn unearthed from the satellite tomb
Height: 47.5cm　Width: 55.6 × 33cm
素面陶钫仓　陪塚 M85 出土
高 47.5　幅 55.6 x 33cm

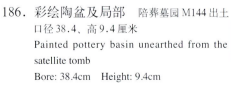

186. 彩绘陶盆及局部　陪葬墓园 M144 出土
口径 38.4、高 9.4 厘米
Painted pottery basin unearthed from the
satellite tomb
Bore: 38.4cm　Height: 9.4cm
彩色陶盆　陪塚 M144 出土
口径 38.4、高 9.4cm

187. **彩绘陶罐（内有粟）** 陪葬墓园M144出土
口径6.5、腹径16、底径8.5、高13厘米
Painted pottery container with millet inside unearthed from
the satellite tomb
Bore: 6.5cm　Belly diameter: 16cm
Bottom diameter: 8.5cm　Height: 13cm
粟を入れた陶缶　陪塚M144出土
口径6.5、腹径16、底径8.5、高13cm

188. **铜甗** 陪葬墓园出土　通高17.3厘米
Bronze cooking vessel unearthed from the satellite tomb
Height: 17.3cm
铜甗　陪塚出土　通高17.3cm

189. 铜龠　陪葬墓园出土　长 10.2、9.4 厘米
Bronze measure unearthed from the satellite tomb
Length: 10.2cm, 9.4cm
銅籥　陪塚 M144 出土　長 10.2、9.4cm

190. 铜质 "周应" 印章
陪葬墓园周应墓出土
高 1.5、边长 2.2 厘米
Bronze seal with inscriptions "Zhouying"
unearthed from Zhouying's Tomb
Height: 1.5cm　Length of each side: 2.2cm
"周応" 銅印章　陪塚周応墓出土
高 1.5、边長 2.2cm

191. 鎏金鸟形铜龠　陪葬墓园出土　高 3.7、宽 5.9 厘米
Gold-plated owl-shaped ornament of dagger-axe unearthed from
the satellite tomb
Height: 3.7cm　Width: 5.9cm
鎏金鳥形人像銅籥　陪塚出土　高 3.7幅、5.9cm

192. 双面人鎏金铜镦
陪葬墓园出土　高 2.2、宽 4.7 厘米
Gold-plated human head ornament of dagger-axe
unearthed from the satellite tomb
Height: 2.2cm　Width: 4.7cm
鎏金両面人像銅飾り　陪塚出土
高 2.2、幅 4.7cm

194. 铜弩机 陪葬墓园出土 高14.7、长9.4、厚4.7厘米
Bronze crossbow trigger unearthed from the satellite tomb
Height: 14.7cm　Length: 9.4cm　Thickness: 4.7cm
銅弩　陪塚出土　高14.7、長9.4、厚4.7cm

195. 四棱铁矛头 南区从葬坑出土 长3.8厘米
Iron spear heads with four blades unearthed from
the satellite tomb
Length: 3.8cm
鉄製の矛先　南区従葬坑出土　長3.8cm

196. 带翼铁镞 陪葬墓园出土 长3.1厘米
Iron arrow heads with wings unearthed from the satellite tomb
Length: 3.1cm
鉄镞　陪塚出土　長3.1cm

193. 铜剑 陪葬墓园出土 长42.3厘米
Bronze sword unearthed from the satellite tomb
Length: 42.3cm
銅剣　陪塚出土　長42.3cm

汉
阳
陵
博
物
馆

197. 鎏金铜承弓器　陪葬墓园出土
长5.1、方孔边长1.2×0.9厘米
Gold-plated crotches for crossbow unearthed from the
satellite tomb
Length: 5.1cm　Length of the square hole: 1.2 x 0.9cm
鎏金銅製弓の支え台　陪塚出土
長5.1　方形穴辺長1.2×0.9cm

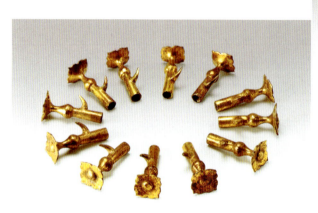

199. 鎏金铜车軎、车辖
陪葬墓园出土
长2.1、直径1.0～2.0厘米
Gold-plated parts of horse and chariot
unearthed from the satellite tomb
Length: 5.1cm　Diameter: 1.0-2.0cm
鎏金銅製車馬具　陪塚出土
長2.1　直径1.0-2.0cm

198. 鎏金铜盖弓帽
陪葬墓园出土　长3.6、帽径1.7厘米
A bunch of gold-plated canopied caps unearthed from the
satellite tomb
Length: 3.6cm　Diameter of the caps: 1.7cm
鎏金車馬具の部品　陪塚出土
長3.6　径1.7cm

200. 鎏金铜双龙纹圆形辔饰
陪葬墓园出土
外径4.1、内径1.9厘米
Round harness ornaments with two gold-plated dragons
unearthed from the satellite tomb
External diameter: 4.1cm
Internal diameter: 1.9cm
鎏金双龍紋円形車馬具　陪塚出土
外径4.1、内径1.9cm

201. 鎏金铜马衔、马镳

陪葬墓园出土　马衔长 7.6、马镳长 7.8 厘米

Gold-plated horse bit and curb unearthed from the satellite tomb

Bit length: 7.6cm　Curb length: 7.8cm

鎏金铜製馬衔、馬镳　陪塚出土　馬衔長 7.6、馬镳長 7.8cm

203. 鎏金带刺铜马衔及象牙镳

陪葬墓园出土　铜马衔长 11.7、镳长 11.3 厘米

Gold-plated horse bit with thorn and ivory horse curb unearthed from the satellite tomb

Bit length: 11.7cm　Curb length: 11.3cm

鎏金铜製馬衔、象牙镳　陪塚出土

馬衔長 11.7、镳長 11.3cm

204. 鎏金铜节约　陪葬墓园出土　高 1.2、径 1.2 厘米

Gold-plated parts of horse and chariot unearthed from the accompanying burial ground

Height: 1.2cm　Diameter: 1.2cm

鎏金铜製節約　陪塚出土　高 1.2、径 1.2cm

202. 鎏金铜达常

陪葬墓园出土　长 12、直径 1.7 厘米

Gold-plated canopy pole unearthed from the satellite tomb

Length: 12cm　Diameter: 1.7cm

鎏金铜製達常　陪塚出土

長 12、直径 1.7cm

205. 鎏金铜兽面　陪葬墓园出土　高 1.3、宽 1.8 厘米

Gold-plated beast ornament unearthed from the satellite tomb

Height: 1.3cm　Width: 1.8cm

鎏金铜製獸面　陪塚出土　高 1.3、幅 1.8cm

206. 鎏金柿蒂纹四乳神兽铜镜　陪葬墓园出土　面径13.4厘米
Gold-plated bronze mirror with four nipples, mythical animal and persimmon design unearthed
from the satellite tomb　Diameter: 13.4cm
鎏金柿紋四乳神獸銅鏡　陪塚出土　直径13.4cm

207. 草叶纹铜镜　陪葬墓园出土　直径11.5厘米
Bronze mirror with leaf design unearthed from the satellite tomb
Diameter: 11.5cm
草葉紋銅鏡　陪塚出土　直径11.5cm

208. 昭明连弧纹铜镜　陪葬墓园出土　直径13.5厘米
Bronze mirror with arc pattern unearthed from the satellite tomb
Diameter: 13.5cm
昭明連弧紋銅鏡　陪塚出土　直径13.5cm

209. 乳丁博局纹铜镜　陪葬墓园出土　直径21.2厘米
Bronze mirror with nipple and chessboard pattern unearthed from
the satellite tomb　Diameter: 21.2cm
乳丁博局紋銅鏡　陪塚出土　直径21.2cm

七、阳陵邑古城遗址

阳陵邑故城遗址位于东区陪葬墓园的东部，东西长4500米，南北宽1000米，总面积4.5平方公里。已探明东西向的街道11条，南北向的街道31条，组成了200余个里坊。主街道宽62米，将陵邑分为南北两个部分。钻探与发掘结果表明北部建筑规模较大且内涵丰富，应为官署区；南部建筑规模较小且遗存简单，应为民居区。在陵邑的南部探明一段970米长的城墙，墙外有护城壕。城内发现有大量的烧造建筑材料和生活用具的陶窑，出土了大量的砖瓦等建筑材料，清理出多处房屋建筑遗迹，且有大量生活用具、封泥、货币等文物出土。阳陵邑作为西汉时期的中小城市，其城内的建筑规模与形制体现出当时全国各地达官显贵、大户豪强不同的建筑等级和风格，是研究西汉陵邑不可缺少的内容。

G. Remains of Yangling County

The county remains of Yangling is located in the eastern part of the eastern satellite tomb with a length of 4,500 meters from east to west and a width of 1,000 meters from south to north, totally 4.5 square kilometers in area. 11 east-west streets and 31 south-north ones have been discovered. Therefore the city consists of over 200 compounds. The main street was 62 meters wide, thus separating the city into two parts. Exploration, drillings and excavations have proved that the northern part has many large-scaled buildings and rich burial objects, indicating it was once the government offices. The southern part has small building remains, and the historical remains are few, inferring it was once the residential area. A 970-meter long city wall with a moat was discovered in the southern part of the city. Many pottery kilns for making building materials and domestic ware were also found, where a large number of building materials such as bricks and tiles were unearthed. Archaeologists also discovered many house remains, domestic ware, sealing clay and coins. As a medium-sized city in that era, Yangling contained buildings with different scales and styles, embodying the nobility and wealth of the high ranking officials and despotic gentries. It is indispensable to study the city of the Han Dynasty.

210. 阳陵邑外景

Yangling County

陽陵邑の外景

7. 陽陵邑古城遺跡

陽陵邑城遺跡は東区陪塚墓園の東部に位置しており、東西の幅は4500メートル、南北の幅は1000メートル、総面積は4.5平方キロメートルである。考古調査によって、東西に並んでいる街道11条、南北の街道が31条ある。主な街道の幅は62メートルあり、陵邑の南と北を分けていた。北部の建築は規模が大きく、豊かな内容を擁し、官庁区であると調査の結果判断された。南部の建築は規模が小さく、遺物も少ないので居住区と判断された。陵邑南部では長さ970メートルの城壁と外堀がある。場内に陶窯が発見され、生活用具やレンガ、瓦など大量の建築材料が出土された。陽陵邑は前漢時代の中等の町で、城内建築の規模と配置から見ると、はっきり当時厳しい等級観念が存在していたことが分かる。この遺跡は、前漢陵邑を研究するための大きな価値を持っている。

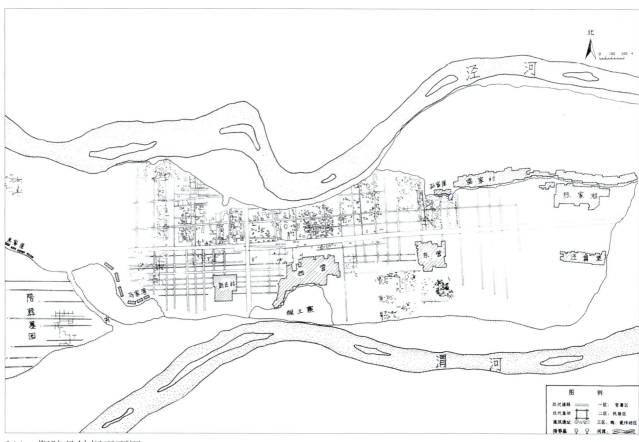

211. 阳陵邑钻探平面图
Excavation map of Yangling County
陽陵邑試掘の平面図

212. 阳陵邑发掘现场
Excavation site of Yangling Cou
陽陵邑の発掘現場

213. "泾置阳陵"瓦当
   Earthenware eaves tile with inscripitions of "Jingzhi
   Yangling"(the Jing River flows by Yangling)
   "泾置陽陵"瓦当

214. "阳陵泾乡"瓦当
   阳陵邑遗址出土　直径14厘米
   Earthenware eaves tile with inscriptions of "Yangling
   Jingxiang" (Yangling lies beyond the Jing River)
   "陽陵泾郷"瓦当

215. "阳陵令印"封泥　阳陵邑遗址出土
   Seal clay of Yangling County governor
   "陽陵令印"封泥

216. 回纹空心砖　阳陵邑遗址出土　长93、宽22.3、厚16.5厘米
Hollow brick with rectangular spirals　unearthed from the Yangling County
Length: 93cm　Width: 22.3cm　Tickness: 16.5cm
回紋空心レンガ　陽陵邑出土　長93、幅22.3、厚16.5cm

217.　阳陵邑发掘的陶窑遗址
Pottery kiln remains unearthed from the Yangling County
陶窯遺跡（2ヶ所）　陽陵邑出土

汉阳陵博物馆

218. 制陶作坊、陶窑
Pottery workshop and pottery kiln
陶窯の発掘現場

219. 陶水井圈　阳陵陵邑遗址出土
Pottery well unearthed from the ruins of
Yangling County
陶製井戸圈　陽陵邑出土

220.汉景帝阳陵陵园远景规划局部示意效果图
Plan map of Yangling Museum
漢景帝陽陵陵園の一部を復元した効果図